A Sunset Book
vegetable gardening

By the editorial staffs of
Sunset Books & Sunset Magazine

contents

Cover photograph by Clyde Childress

Twenty-second Printing May 1974

TITLE NO. 380

LANE BOOKS
Menlo Park, California

vegetable gardening ... some new concepts

A new kind of home vegetable garden is taking over from the spacious row-on-row plots we have been accustomed to in the past. Because so many of today's houses are built on small lots, vegetable gardens must be planned more compactly. Emphasis is swinging away from quantity into the direction of fun, experimentation, and informality.

VEGETABLES IN SMALL GARDENS

The gardener with limited space has no desire to turn his entire yard into a growing ground for vegetables. He wants his family to enjoy the benefits of a patio, a children's play area, several flower beds, some grass, a few small trees, and perhaps an "extra" or two, such as a drying yard, a garden work center, or a dog-run.

We have written this book with the small-space gardener very much in mind, hoping that he will include a few vegetables somewhere in his landscaping scheme. The realm of gardening, with all of its fascinating aspects, offers no experience more satisfying than that of entering the kitchen with an armload of fresh, delectable vegetables from the garden. To miss out on this opportunity in the mistaken belief that raising vegetables is passé is to deny yourself one of gardening's greatest pleasures.

As evidenced in the landscaping chapter, there are innumerable situations in which you can raise vegetables—in borders, raised beds, tubs, open spaces in paved areas, along paths and walkways, interplanted with flowers. All but the smallest gardens can provide room for something similar to the 15-by-20-foot plot shown on page 18.

HOW ABOUT FLAVOR?

Even though growing your own vegetables is satisfying and fun, there would be little point to it if the results of your labors turned out to be mediocre table fare. Here we come to a happy fact: *The tastiest vegetables are the ones you grow at home and serve fresh from the garden.*

The freshness factor is more important with some vegetables than with others. For example, winter squash, potatoes, and dry onions are grown to be harvested, stored for a reasonable length of time, and used as needed. Market-purchased varieties of these vegetables are excellent, and there is little point to growing them unless you have plenty of space. On the other hand, a vine-ripened tomato is far superior to anything you'll find at the store. Fresh lettuce is outstanding. Peas and sweet corn, eaten minutes after picking and before most of their sugar content has turned to starch, completely outclass the market fare.

The steady development of new varieties of vegetables during recent years has been nothing short of phenomenal. To the benefit of the home gardener and the commercial grower, many diseases have been conquered, growing limits increased, and yields multiplied.

In this book, intended for home gardeners only, the recommended varieties were selected with flavor uppermost in mind. Our lists represent only a sampling; there are many hundreds of fine home garden varieties, and it is wise (as well as fun) to send for several seed company catalogs. Many varieties do better in some regions than others. Your local nurseryman is your best source of information as to what vegetables and varieties you should grow.

THE ECONOMY FACTOR

Is it possible to save money by growing your own vegetables? Maybe and maybe not, depending on what and how much you grow.

We've known gardeners who could sit down and figure out almost to the dollar what their vegetable garden saved them each year on the food bill—and an impressive total it was, too. (Opportunities for economizing are greatest if you have a freezer; surpluses can be used throughout the year.)

Looking at the other extreme (with tongue in cheek) we recall a gardening friend who, after growing a small crop of corn under rather poor conditions, figured he would have to put a price tag of 50 cents an ear on the end product in order to break even!

The truth here is probably somewhere in the middle; you will save a few dollars a month at best, and come out about even at the worst. But in terms of pleasure and taste, you're always ahead.

the fundamentals

To produce vegetables a good cut in quality above those you can buy at the store, you must understand one basic, elementary fact: The *minute a vegetable plant stops growing, it's in trouble.* Unlike most flowers, vegetables seldom fully recover if growth is checked. Making them grow fast, forcing them through to maturity, is the key to the full basket at harvest time.

No vegetable grows well in full shade. No vegetable thrives in poor soil. No vegetable is drought-resistant.

Every vegetable, from artichoke to zucchini, demands sun (in most cases, *full* sun), rich soil, and a regular and generous watering program. But in a fourth and very important requirement — growing heat — there are substantial differences between classes of vegetables and between individual kinds.

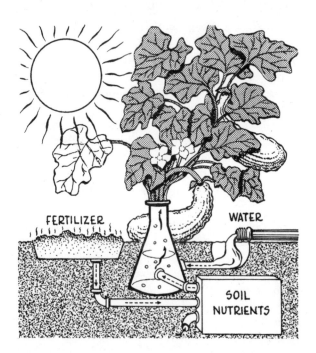

FERTILIZER · WATER · SOIL NUTRIENTS

WARM AND COOL-SEASON VEGETABLES

You, the gardener, can supply water, modify soil, and plant the garden where it will get adequate sunlight. Therefore, temperature, which is largely out of your hands, becomes the most im-

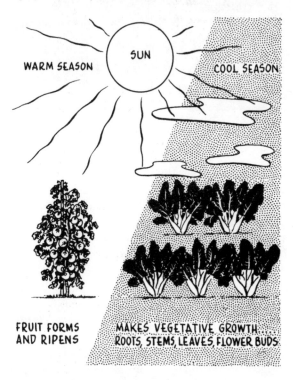

WARM SEASON · SUN · COOL SEASON

FRUIT FORMS AND RIPENS · MAKES VEGETATIVE GROWTH: ROOTS, STEMS, LEAVES, FLOWER BUDS

portant single consideration in deciding which vegetables you can grow well and what time of year you must plant them.

WARM-SEASON CROPS

The summer or warm-season vegetables require soil warmth to germinate, and long days and high temperatures both day and night if they are to form and ripen fruit. With most warm-season vegetables, the *fruit* is the object of the harvest rather than the *leaves*, *roots*, or *stems*.

The standard seed packet phrase, "sow when all danger of frost is past," explains the temperature factor only on the basis of tenderness to frost. The other temperature factor is the basic need of warm weather vegetables for *adequate growing heat* to keep them moving along unchecked and to ripen their crops. It is perfectly possible to set out beans, eggplants, or tomatoes well after the last frost, but you will watch them simply mark time until the heat they require to move along is available.

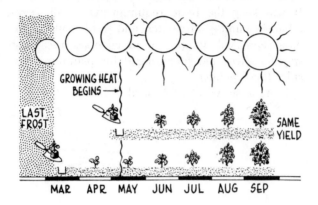

In some cool coastal areas, there are no frosts at all, yet many warm-weather crops simply cannot be grown because there isn't enough available growing heat during the summer to mature them. Conversely, in very hot areas only a few kinds of vegetables will survive summer dog days.

Planting time for warm-weather vegetables should be not only "after danger of frost is past" but also after the soil has lost its winter clamminess and has begun to warm up. This date varies according to region and its climate.

Here are some common warm-season vegetables, arranged approximately from lowest to highest in heat requirements: snap beans, summer squash, tomatoes, cucumbers, winter squash and pumpkins, corn, okra, muskmelons, peppers, lima beans, eggplants, casaba melons, watermelons.

Whether you choose an early or a late-maturing variety of the vegetable you wish to grow can often be the difference between success and failure. For a discussion of this subject, see pages 10 and 11.

COOL-SEASON CROPS

The cool-season vegetables make steady growth at average temperatures 10° or 15° below those necessary for warm-season crops. In addition many of them — cabbage, for example — will recover from moderately heavy frost.

The gardeners who live in mild climate areas are able to grow and harvest winter vegetables during the cool months of the year. Leaf and root vegetables flourish in fall and winter when insect pests are few and soil moisture is plentiful. (Peas are a fruiting crop with a definite temperature ceiling that limits them to the cool side of the calendar.)

We harvest carrots and other *root* crops midway in their development. Likewise, we harvest *leaves* of chard, lettuce, and cabbage; *stems* of rhubarb and asparagus; *immature flowers* of cauliflower, broccoli, and artichoke before they flower and set seed.

Two environmental factors that trigger flower and seed production, causing the plant to "bolt," are rising temperatures and lengthening days. Short days and cool weather, on the other hand, channel its energies into vegetative functions: forming leaves, roots, stems, and immature flower heads.

Success or failure with most cool-weather vegetables depends to a large extent on how well you schedule plantings to bring them up to size in the kind of weather that makes for vegetative growth rather than for flowering. In general, the object is to plant very early in spring so the crop matures before summer heat arrives, or in late summer so the crop comes in during the cool days of fall.

VEGETABLES ARE A CLANNISH BUNCH

Later in this book you will find how-to-grow-it information on each of the vegetables that are most commonly grown in home gardens. They are listed in alphabetical order so that the reader will be able to find what he's looking for quickly and easily.

However, to fully understand vegetables it is necessary to know the various families they belong to. Generally, the *basic* cultural needs of the vegetables within a given family are the same. You will notice, for instance, that all of the root crops are cool-season growers, all vine crops are warm-season growers, etc.

Here is a brief survey of common garden vegetables by classes and kinds:

Perennials: Artichoke, asparagus, rhubarb. All three are cool-season crops. Generally thought of as "luxury" vegetables, they are frequently grown as part of the ornamental garden for decorative use as well as for the crop. One planting will bear for many years.

Leaf crops: Celery, chard, lettuce, mustard, parsley, spinach. All are cool-season crops. Under this heading, you go from the very easy and very desirable home garden plants (chard, lettuce, mustard) to two crops that are so challenging that few find growing them worthwhile. Spinach and celery are in the challenging class (most gardeners would rather buy them at the store).

Root crops: Beets, carrots, onions, parsnips, radishes, salsify, sweet potatoes, turnips and rutabagas, white potatoes. All are cool-season crops except sweet potatoes. Root vegetables, except potatoes, return the highest poundage per square foot, with the possible exception of kale. Potatoes, white or sweet, are only for the gardener with lots of space. All root crops like a loose, well-spaded soil that will not inhibit the edible roots as they grow down into the soil.

Cole crops, or cabbage family: Broccoli, Brussels sprouts, cabbage, cauliflower, collards, kale, kohlrabi. All are cool-season growers. Cole crops are heavy feeders that benefit from side dressings of plant food during the growing season. Best all-around member of the cole crops for home gardens is broccoli, with its long harvest period.

The legumes: Snap beans, lima beans, peas, and "Southern peas" or "cowpeas" such as blackeyes. Most of them are available in both bush and pole (climbing) types. Snap beans, Southern peas, and limas are warm-season crops. Southern peas (technically beans) require considerable summer heat to mature. Snap beans are among the best of all crops for the home garden. Lima beans and peas are also excellent, but they are a little fussier as to climate. Bush types of these vegetables make it possible to grow them in even the smallest of gardens.

Vine crops or cucurbit family: Cucumbers, late melons, muskmelons, pumpkins, squash, watermelons. All are warm-season growers. All of the cucurbits are very heavy feeders. Most of them are space-consumers, although cucumbers can be trained on trellises. Most summer squashes are so wonderfully productive that you need only a few plants.

The solanaceous fruits: Tomato, eggplant, and pepper are all warm-season vegetables. Tomatoes are a particular favorite of home gardeners everywhere. All you need are a few plants of any of these vegetables to give you an ample harvest. They are among the most popular vegetables sold by nurseries as young transplants.

Corn and okra are "loners" that don't fit any of the 7 main categories. Both are warm-season crops. Corn is a very popular home garden vegetable in many sections of the country, but is not productive enough to rank as a favorite for small gardens. Okra is popular in the South and warm Southwest, but is seldom grown in other regions.

PRE-PLANTING "MUSTS"

If you keep the basic requirements of all vegetables in mind — sun, water, and fertile soil — common sense will guide you in choosing the right spot for them and preparing it for planting. Consider these points:

1. Because vegetables need full sun, the plot should be far enough from trees or structures to avoid their shade. If one end of the plot gets more sun than the other, plant fruiting crops there, leaf and root crops where shade creeps in part of the day.

Tree roots, too, compete with vegetables for water and nutrients. As a rule-of-thumb, for helping to determine how far away from the tree you should plant, remember this: a tree's roots generally spread out about as far as its branches. If you must put the leaf and root crops in a place where

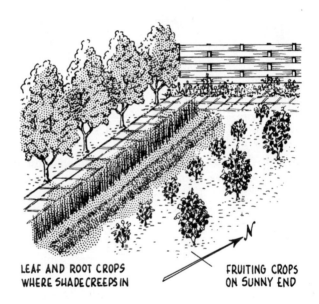

LEAF AND ROOT CROPS
WHERE SHADE CREEPS IN

FRUITING CROPS
ON SUNNY END

tree roots will compete with them, double up on the amount of fertilizer and water that you give to those crops.

2. A level site is better than a sloping one, since water goes down into the soil instead of running off. If your garden is on a slope, plant vegetables in a shelf or contour furrow so you can flood the root area.

3. Because vegetables are fast-growing and hungry, they need nutrients in quantity. Weed-free manure is still one of the best soil conditioners for vegetables. Work it in at planting time. The perfect

soil for vegetables is a loose, fertile, well-drained loam. Soil building techniques you use elsewhere in the garden apply to vegetables as well; vegetables are, if anything, *more* demanding in soil requirements than other plants.

STIRRING UP ADOBE OR CLAY SOIL WITH POWER CULTIVATOR ISN'T ENOUGH

YOU HAVE TO ADD HUMUS MATERIALS...

COMPOST

PEAT

SAWDUST

ROTTED MANURE

FIR BARK

LEAF MOLD

Although most vegetables will tolerate slight alkalinity, they fail or do poorly in acid soil. If you suspect that your soil is acid, try growing a few beets; if they show ragged or stunted growth, an excess in soil acidity is indicated. Agricultural lime, available in nurseries in acid-soil sections of the country, is the best means of counteracting acidity. Lime does more than "sweeten" or neutralize the soil; it helps to release for plant use such vital elements as phosphorous and potash that might otherwise lie latent and unused.

4. Soil should be thoroughly moist 2 or 3 feet down, at planting time — not *after* you plant, but before. In dry areas this means diking up sections of the garden-to-be, raising 8-inch ridges in squares 6 feet or more each way, then flooding them, allowing water to sink down, and flooding again. Soil should then be allowed to dry slightly until it's workable, especially if it's high in clay. If it balls up when you squeeze a handful, it's too wet; if it crumbles, it's right. Water stored in the soil when you plant should be sufficient to germinate most kinds of seed — an important point, since sprinkling afterwards to make up for moisture deficiencies often washes out new seed or forms a hard crust over it.

WATERING

Overhead watering suits most of the cool-season crops very well. To a degree, it simulates the fog that goes with the cool air along the coast where these plants grow so well. It is a wonderfully easy method for the home gardener, who has but to place his lawn sprinkler where it can gradually and evenly water the vegetables. On the other hand, overhead watering can damage many hot-weather crops, especially squash and the other vine crops (makes ideal conditions for mildew) and tomatoes (causes skins to crack).

Surface watering: Most vegetables are rather shallow-rooted and therefore suffer quickly in dry periods. The most common error in irrigation technique is irregularity in amount of water and in timing. Alternate wet and very dry periods seriously affect many vegetables. Overwatering is often harmful. Every effort should be made to maintain a uniform moisture supply during the growing season. During the seedling stage, the top 2 inches should be moist. Later on, the top 2-inch layer can be dry but the lower 10 should be kept moist. Inspect your soil regularly with a spade.

Even a small-plot gardener is wise to select surface irrigation as his method of applying water. When a variety of vegetables is crowded into a small area, overhead sprinkling cannot be selective enough to avoid vegetables that resent water on their foliage or fruit. Also, it is too easy to underwater if the sprinkler is in the hands of an impatient human. Most important is the fact that irrigation can be applied without soaking the top dust mulch covering the soil, and thus saves water and the task of cultivating the entire surface of the garden after watering.

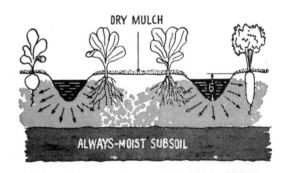

DRY MULCH

ALWAYS-MOIST SUBSOIL

In laying out your irrigation system keep the furrows as level as possible. Too much of a drop will cause the water to flow too rapidly to properly penetrate the soil. Good gardeners know that it takes time to do a thorough job of irrigation. Check-dams, built with board, soil, or shovel, slow up the flow of the water and allow it to seep deeply into the soil. Be careful that the force of water from the

hose does not dig into the soil; let it run into a small tub or box, or tie a sack or a piece of canvas over the open end of the hose.

If you plan to go away for a vacation, it is absolutely essential that you make arrangements for someone to keep the vegetables watered during your absence. One summer hot spell — even for a single day — can wreck an entire vegetable garden if the plants fail to get water. If you can, make it easy for whoever is to take over the watering task. One way is to arrange irrigation systems that are near automatic. In small plots ditch systems can be arranged so that only one or two changes in position of the hose will water the plot.

WEEDING AND CULTIVATING

Weeds have no place among vegetables because they take more nutrients and water from the root area than you might think. Hoe them out as soon as they appear. It is best to scrape instead of chop; *don't dig in deep or you'll ruin the hard-working feeder roots.* Water and nutrients enter roots through the growing root tips — often just beneath the surface.

MULCHING

Mulches cut down on the frequency of watering and weeding. Apply the mulch after the plants are well above ground and after the soil is warm. Make the mulch blanket at least 2 inches thick. Many materials can be used as mulches, and, after the growth season, they are spaded into the soil. Clean straw, wood shavings, sawdust, leaf mold, and processed manure require the expenditure of a few dollars, but used as water savers in summer and finally as soil conditioners they pay for themselves.

New sawdust and shavings use much nitrogen at first stages of rotting. To prevent plant roots from being robbed of nitrogen, scatter ammonium sulphate or urea before applying the mulch.

In recent years, black-pigmented polyethylene film has shown great promise as an effective "mulch" for home vegetable gardens. Fruits and vegetables that tend to rot when in contact with wet soil — strawberries, melons, squash, unstaked tomatoes — will produce more and cleaner crops if mulched with black plastic. (See chapter on squash.)

FERTILIZING

All vegetables are heavy feeders. If your soil is naturally rich in nutrients, you are fortunate, but even if this is true you will sooner or later find that it is necessary to give the soil an occasional nutritional boost.

The quickest and most efficient way to correct plant food deficiencies in the soil is through the addition of commercial fertilizers. They contain the 3 most important chemical elements — nitrogen, phosphorus, and potash. For row crops, it is most convenient to apply the fertilizer prior to planting, in bands 3 to 4 inches from the plants and 3 to 4 inches deep. For the proper amount to apply, follow the label directions for whatever kind of fertilizer you happen to prefer. If you use liquid fertilizer, mix and apply according to directions, and apply it as a drench. Wash it off plant foliage.

Best results will be obtained by using light fertilizer applications at frequent intervals rather than a heavy dose at one time. When plants are sizeable, fertilizing by side dressing or adding plant foods to irrigation water is most practical.

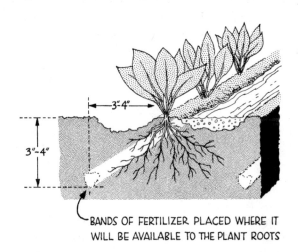

BANDS OF FERTILIZER PLACED WHERE IT WILL BE AVAILABLE TO THE PLANT ROOTS

The most inexpensive way to build up your soil is to add compost. However, although it is true that well-made compost can be a boon to any gardener, it is also true that compost bins are becoming more and more scarce in today's home gardens. The principal reason: *They can breed flies!* There are other reasons, too, such as the offensive odors that can be wafted into your window (or your neighbor's window) from a poorly tended compost pile. Weeds, plant pests, and diseases are spread around by material from improperly managed composts. The small lots which are typical of so many of today's subdivision homes are frequently ill-suited to a composting area.

INSECTS AND DISEASES

One worthy goal in home vegetable growing is to bring a crop to harvest without spraying or dusting. The reason for this goal is obvious. If no poison of any kind has ever been on your vegetables, you have little to wash off (just dust or mud) and even less to worry about.

The first weapon in this non-chemical warfare is the garden hose. A hard jet of water will knock off and banish many an insect invasion.

Hand-picking is another effective pest control method. If you see a big worm or two (or two dozen) eating your plants, pick them off, put them in a bag or can, and throw the container into the garbage. If leaves are being chewed but you can't find the culprits in the daytime, go out and inspect your plants with a flashlight at night. Pick off and throw away any creatures you find.

Most common night-feeding pests are cutworms, snails, slugs, and earwigs. To combat these, there are poison baits that you can place in your garden but *not* on the plants, thus eliminating the pests without coming in contact with the vegetables.

But there are times when pests are doing damage to a crop and neither the water-squirt, the day-and-night search, nor the placing of poison baits will do any good. Then (and only then) you must fall back on spraying or dusting with an insecticide or miticide.

For your guidance in recognizing insecticide and miticide chemicals when you see their names on labels, here are some of the most common:

Rotenone, pyrethrum: These are non-poisonous to man and therefore can be used closer to harvest time than other insecticides. They are not persistent, which means that you can use them without indirectly causing damage to wildlife. They control a few of the common sucking and chewing insects.

Nicotine sulfate: Like pyrethrum and rotenone, it offers no hazard to wildlife by indirect action, but it is highly toxic to man as it comes from the bottle. *Use with extreme care.*

Diazinon, guthion, malathion, sevin: These insect and mite-killing chemicals are completely manufactured (the three mentioned above, by contrast, are extracted from plants). They are safe to use on vegetables *if* the label says so (there are different kinds of formulations—some safe on edibles, some not) and *if* you follow label instructions to the letter!

Aldrin, chlordane, DDD, DDT, dieldrin, endrin, heptachlor, kelthane, lindane, tedion, toxaphene: These are all chlorinated hydrocarbons which share, in varying degrees, one characteristic—they break down slowly or not at all, in contrast to most other insecticides which change into harmless substances within hours or days of application. Frequently, the chlorinated hydrocarbons eventually break down into chemicals which are just as toxic as was the original. Because of this long-term destructive chemical potency, no chlorinated hydrocarbon products should be used in your garden.

Methoxychlor: Strangely, although this is a chlorinated hydrocarbon and the other chlorinated hydrocarbon insecticides (see above) are known to be persistent and therefore hazardous, this one is not persistent. There is no record of its killing non-target organisms (birds, fish), and no record of its accumulating in man's tissues as the other chlorinated hydrocarbons are doing. Therefore, it is theoretically safe to use methoxychlor on vegetables. It is packaged and labeled for that use. However, use it only if you can't find another recommended insecticide.

Vegetables can also fall prey to certain plant diseases, blights, and fungi. Disinfectants, used to treat seeds and soil alike, are widely available and quite effective. Proper culture is also important; a healthy vegetable plant can resist disease better than a weak and spindly one. If you find any badly diseased plants in your garden — vegetables or otherwise — pull them and burn them immediately so that their infectious spores will not spread to other parts of the garden.

which vegetables are for you?

There is nothing more futile than trying to tell a dedicated vegetable gardener that he should not or cannot grow such-and-such a crop. Even if his soil and climate conditions are all wrong, chances are better than fair that he can make a liar out of you — if he really wants to. Modern methods of soil improvement, insect and disease control, and hybridizing have brought about so many improvements that almost anything is possible.

However, as far as the typical weekend home gardener is concerned, there are definite considerations and limitations which — if he knows them and heeds them — permit him to raise vegetables with a maximum of enjoyment and a minimum of fuss and bother. Here are the most important ones:

1. Choose vegetables you like. Select varieties your family likes, and concentrate on the kinds that are markedly better when harvested fresh from the garden, such as tomatoes, carrots, snap beans, corn, and muskmelons.

2. Consider maintenance time. Some vegetables are extremely easy to grow, others demand more care. Chard is very easy and bears over a long period. Four plants take the space you would allow a rose bush. Rhubarb and artichoke have ornamental value and will bear for several seasons from a single planting. A 30-foot row of asparagus will give you something to look forward to every spring for years, with negligible maintenance.

3. Select varieties carefully. According to the catalog, they're all good; but they aren't — in all climates. Some will do fine in many regions, but will succumb to disease in other locations. Earliness or lateness of the variety can be very important (see pages 10 and 11). Your nurseryman or county agent can give you sound suggestions about best varieties for your area.

4. Use space well. Root crops and leafy vegetables provide the biggest yields in the smallest space. Beans, tomatoes, cucumbers, or any other crops that you can train upward will, in this manner, occupy

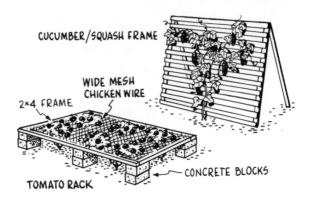

only a fraction of the space that they would require if allowed to sprawl on the ground.

5. Consider length of harvest period. If you're going to eat them fresh, vegetables that you can harvest over a long period are better for home gardens than those that come in all at once. You can harvest carrots for months, but turnips get woody if left in the ground too long. You can continue to harvest small heads of sprouting broccoli for many weeks, while cabbage should be picked at maturity.

6. Plant for use. You'll need only a small plot to provide ample fresh produce through the summer. With a larger plot, you'd better have plans for the surplus. Tomatoes from more than six plants are likely to go to waste in an average family unless you can them. It makes little sense to grow more than a few eggplants, since no one has yet discovered a way to preserve them really well. In almost every home vegetable garden, there's a row or two of lettuce that goes to seed in midsummer. The space it occupied could have been used more wisely for carrots or chard.

If you have a freezer, most vegetable surplus can be frozen. Crops like snap beans and summer squash, which mature all at once, can be harvested in awesome quantities. Of course, it's wise to concentrate on vegetables that freeze best. Yellow crookneck squash, for example, makes a better frozen product than zucchini. (For detailed information, see the freezing chart on page 65.)

seed packet know-how

It is possible for a flower gardener to tend his garden for years, and never grow a single plant from seed. Many gardeners would prefer to pay a few dollars for several dozen nursery-grown annual seedlings, and save themselves the "trouble" of planting their own seeds.

This is not true of vegetable gardeners. Some vegetables, such as peppers, tomatoes, and cabbage, are frequently purchased from nurseries because it takes only a few to suit your needs. However, many kinds of vegetables cannot be transplanted easily and are nearly always grown from seed sown directly in the soil where they are to grow; beans, carrots, sweet corn, and spinach are just a few.

Dyed-in-the-wool seed enthusiasts prefer to grow *all* of their crops from seed. During the winter months when other gardeners are peering out of their windows and waiting for spring, the seed fancier is sowing seeds in anticipation of the time when frosts will end and transplanting will begin. It is true that by doing so, he is probably saving himself a few dollars. Much more important, he will be growing varieties that are selected and marketed in packets by the seed companies with an eye to their fresh-flavor quality and home garden adaptability. (Nursery-grown transplants are usually excellent, but the number of varieties offered is limited.)

Many of the vegetables you find in today's markets are varieties which have been developed principally for shipping and storage qualities rather than taste. They must be able to keep without spoiling for weeks, and they must have special qualities which permit them to be packed and shipped for long distances. This is not to say that just because a vegetable variety is a commercial favorite it should be ruled out for home gardeners — some of the top home varieties and market varieties are one and the same. Nevertheless, the seeds available in packets to home gardeners represent the very finest-tasting vegetables available.

WHICH VARIETY TO CHOOSE?

Choosing the right vegetable variety is basic to both production and quality of crop. In many climates, variety makes the difference between bumper harvest and outright failure. Seed of new hybrids costs little more than that of older ones, and you're missing a bet if you don't take advantage of the tremendous research effort the seed companies and state college experiment stations are putting into development of new disease-resistant, highly productive strains, tailor-made for a variety of climatic conditions.

In the section of this book which discusses the characteristics and cultural requirements of the leading home garden vegetables, you will find names of some recommended varieties. By no means should these selections be considered to be the last word as to what kinds you should try. What they do represent is a carefully assembled sampling of some of those varieties that crop up time and again on the "recommended" lists of seed companies and agricultural extension services throughout the country.

"EARLY" AND "LATE" VARIETIES

Early varieties require less heat and late varieties more heat to mature. Number of days from seed to maturity, usually specified in the catalog or on the seed packet, is an important clue for the cool climate gardener who wants to grow warm-season crops. *Figures are based on ideal conditions.* As available heat in his own garden falls below the ideal, the number of days required to mature the crop increases.

An early corn, for example, may be listed at 60 days, which is approximate seed-to-harvest time in California's warm Sacramento Valley. It may require 80 days to mature in Salem, Oregon, and 100 days in Bellingham, Washington. In either of the latter two cool-climate areas, gardeners are better off with an early corn than with a very late one, since it's possible the late variety might never receive the amount of total heat it needs to mature properly.

On the other hand, if there's more than enough total heat available, plant early varieties only at the very beginning of the season so they will be almost ready for harvest before really hot weather sets in. If an early 60-day tomato is planted in California's Imperial Valley in December or January (under paper caps), it might mature a good crop in March. Planted in late spring, however, it might mature in 50 days or less; vines would be under-developed with fruit small and sunburned. The same early tomato might be planted in Seattle in May, take 80 or more days to ripen, and bear high quality fruit.

Early summer vegetables, then, are valuable to the hot climate gardener who wants an early harvest, and to the cool climate gardener who might not be able to mature the late varieties at all because of their heat requirements.

SOWING SEEDS OUTDOORS

The timing of your plantings and seed sowing instructions are discussed later in this book, under each separate kind of vegetable. These directions give you the necessary precautions to take in certain instances, such as in the case of the slow-germinating carrot seed or the easily-rotted bean.

You may be bothered somewhat by the briefness of vegetable seed packet instructions. By necessity a seed packet must be directed to all climates and it must leave much unsaid. One always-helpful piece of information to be found on a seed packet is the amount of seed to sow per foot of row. In following those directions you can safely thin down on the amount of seed used.

In sowing seed it is best not to shake the seed from the packet; instead, hold a small supply in the palm of your hand and sow by rolling seeds out from between the thumb and forefinger of the other hand. There are excellent plant hormone preparations available at nurseries and garden stores for stimulation of root growth from seeds and after transplanting. Simply dust the seed with the preparation according to label directions.

Soil should be deeply soaked *before* seeds are planted, and then allowed to dry just enough so it is loose and friable.

NEW WAYS TO START SEEDS

Several paragraphs farther on, you will find a step-by-step procedure for sowing seed in flats. The seed-flat method, along with the time-honored methods of starting seeds in pots and in plant bands, is excellent and we recommend it highly. However, several exciting and immensely practical new products have come into being in very recent years which make it easy for the most inexperienced beginner to start seeds indoors.

For example, there are seed starter kits for tomatoes and certain other vegetables (also for annuals). All you do is remove the lid of the container (or punch holes in it), and water. Seed, humus, and nutrients may all be in the container, or the seed may be in a separate packet so you can sow it yourself. The seeding medium is virtually sterile, so you don't have to worry about damping-off, the fungus disease that often attacks seedlings a few days after they have poked their way through the soil, causing them to wilt and die.

In a few weeks you will have 2 to 3 dozen plants to prick out in pots, transplanting flats, or into the gar-

den. The kits are attractively packaged with easy-to-follow directions. It is best to transplant seedlings before they become large and woody.

One of the "fringe benefits" of starter kits is the fascination they hold for children. We know of no better way to introduce a youngster to the world of plants.

Among the most popular of the new seed-starter products are the tiny pots made of compressed peat moss, manure, or other material such as cellulose.

You fill them with good soil and put a seed or two (or a small seedling) in each one. Then when the seedlings are large enough to transplant, you plant pot and all. Roots grow right through walls of the pot, and the plants don't suffer transplanting shock. You also don't lose any soil from around the roots, as so frequently happens when you dig plants out of a flat or a pot. Nutrients are built into the pot

walls and carry the seedlings along during the early stages of growth.

Starter kits and compressed peat pots do best when kept by a warm, sunny window.

SOWING SEEDS IN FLATS

Starting plants in flats is still the best-known and most widely practiced method used by home gardeners. A seed flat is any shallow box used for starting seeds. The size used by most gardeners is 14 inches wide by 24 inches long, and from 3 to 4 inches deep; smaller "pony" flats supply the needs of many of today's smaller-sized gardens. Flats need cracks or holes in the bottom for drainage.

Here is an excellent method for sowing seeds in flats:

1. Make up a loose seeding mixture of 1 part loam, 1 part clean sand or Perlite, and 1 part leaf mold or moist peat. (Screen the leaf mold or peat before adding it.) You can use sifted sphagnum moss or Vermiculite instead of this mixture, if you like. Also, packaged potting soil, all mixed and ready to use, is now available in many areas in 25-pound sacks with carrying handles. This is another development to save you the time and bother of making up small quantities of potting soil when you don't have all the necessary raw materials on hand.

2. Sift the seeding mix into the flat, working it down into the corners with your fingers. (Commercial growers often line the bottom of the flat with a layer of newspaper so the mix won't trickle out through the open spaces between boards.) Firm the seeding mix with a block of wood (a "float"). Make sure the soil surface is level. When firmed, the seeding mix should be ½ inch below top of flat.

3. Soak the filled flat in water. Let it drain.

4. If the seed has not been pretreated with a fungicide such as captan, semesan, or spergon, you can treat it in the seed packet by tearing off one corner, dropping in the specified amount of disinfectant, then shaking the packet to coat each seed. Treating the seeds will help prevent damping-off.

5. Sow tiny seeds over the seedbed, and press them gently into the surface with a block of wood

or a float. Don't cover them. Sow medium-sized seeds in shallow furrows pressed into the soil. Furrows should be the depth you intend to plant seed, and 2 inches apart. Cover with sifted sphagnum,

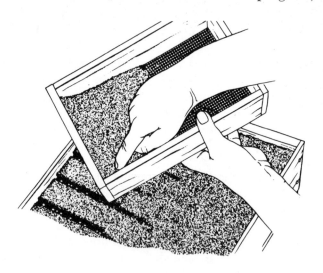

sand, or Vermiculite, and press firm with the float. If the seeds are very large, you can poke them into the seeding mix with your fingers, and then cover them.

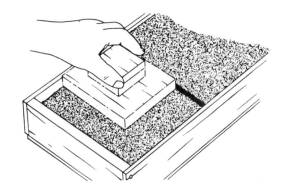

6. Cover the flat with a pane of glass and a sheet of newspaper, or just a double sheet of newspaper.

Set the flat in a warm, light spot, but not in direct sunlight. Check daily to see that the seeding mix doesn't dry out, and remove the paper or glass when the seeds germinate.

7. Give plants more light as growth progresses. Seedlings get spindly if grown too warm; they do best at about 60°. Carefully transplant the seedlings to another flat when two sets of true leaves have developed. Some gardeners water them in with a transplanting solution that eases the shock and keeps the plants growing vigorously; whether or not you use a transplanting solution, it is important to water in the transplanted seedlings and maintain a constant moisture all the time they are growing in the flat. The mixture in the transplanting flat should contain 2 parts loam to 1 part sand and 1 part sifted leaf mold or pre-moistened peat.

8. Set the young seedlings in the garden several weeks later, at planting time. Don't keep putting it off, or their growth will be checked as they become "flatbound."

THINNING

Whether you sow seeds directly where they are to grow or indoors in containers, never be timid about thinning. (When a seed packet contains information on how many feet of row the contents will sow, the casualty rate from thinnings has been taken into account.) It is generally best to thin before seedlings are over 2 inches tall and before roots become intertwined. Follow spacing directions on the seed packets.

Thinnings need not always be thrown away. Very young lettuce is a superior salad item, and baby carrots are a gourmet treat. Or, you may be able to transplant the thinnings.

TRANSPLANTING

Every effort should be made to avoid root disturbance in transplanting. If seedlings are in flats, the soil should be blocked out (cut in squares) when the seedlings are moved. If planted in pots, water by soaking the night before and tap the soil ball out by turning upside-down and tapping the bottom of the pot or striking its edge against the corner of a bench. If planted in paper cups or cardboard, cut the side and remove the paper.

Some of the vegetables that transplant easily are: beets, broccoli, cabbage, cauliflower, celery, chard, eggplant, kale, lettuce, peppers, tomatoes. Turnips and carrots should be sown directly in the ground; beets can be transplanted when small, but usually are sown where they are to grow. Beans, peas, melons, cucumbers, and squash can be transplanted only when soil is not disturbed around their roots. Plant the seed in small pots, paper containers, or plant bands; better yet, use compressed peat pots.

It is always best to transplant in the cool of late afternoon or early evening. If the job must be done in the warm sunlight, give the plants the temporary shade of a shingle or paper.

When transplanting, never make the mistake of compressing the soil tightly at the base of the plant. Firm the soil just enough so that the plant will have a good footing and roots will be able to spread out into loose, friable soil.

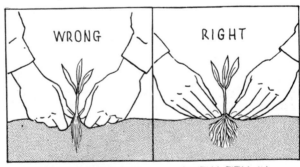

DON'T SQUEEZE ROOTS INTO A TIGHT BALL   GENTLY FIRM IN YOUR PLANTS

the most popular planting systems

The basic theories behind any planting pattern are to make it easy to get water into the root zone without waste and to simplify cultivation and make weed control less time consuming. The following systems are time-proven, and you will find them in vegetable gardens everywhere:

DOUBLE ROW PLANTING

Planting small vegetables (root crops, onions) in double rows a few inches from the furrow edge is the classic commercial system. It makes irrigation and cultivation simple for the commercial grower.

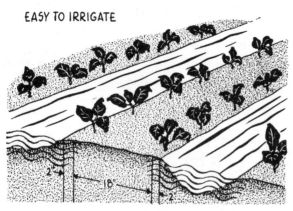

EASY TO IRRIGATE

However, it's hard to see its advantages for the home gardener. Of course, high, double row planting makes for better drainage in areas where rains are heavy. And if your garden is very long and narrow, with different crops strung out like beads on a string, you can irrigate it very simply. These are the disadvantages: In light, sandy soils, furrows fill in after a couple of irrigations, and no matter how long the water runs, there is very little lateral movement; it goes straight down. In hot climates, plants set high dry out much faster than they would on the flat ground.

FLAT PLANTING

Flat planting is a perfectly sound practice unless flooding from rains is a hazard. Soil doesn't dry out as readily as it does under the double row system. If you irrigate, raise low ridges with the hoe before watering. Most home gardeners who plant on the flat use sprinklers, letting them spray gently so water will seep into the soil slowly and thoroughly.

EASY SPRINKLING

RAISED BEDS

Where spring and summer rainfall is heavy, raised or "Dutch" beds are useful. Furrows are cut one foot deep; excavated soil is used for raised beds. Furrows lead to a drainage ditch at the end of the garden; they carry off excess moisture. Raised beds dry off faster and warm up earlier than flat plantings.

FURROW PLANTING

The single row and furrow pattern is simply a 6-inch, V-shaped ditch made with the hoe. Seed is sown along one shoulder, just below the top. Furrows should be spaced far enough apart to give roots plenty of growing space between. If the furrow runs east and west, the south side of the furrow will receive full benefit of the sun.

Virtually all crops, small or large, can be grown in this manner. As plants develop, move the furrows outward.

HILL PLANTING

Hill planting does not mean making mounds; it means grouping seeds so 3 or 4 plants grow in a cluster a foot or more in diameter, either on the flat or along a furrow. The theory is that roots range out from a central point and get more foraging room in the soil. Big crops — squash, corn, melons, and pole beans — are sometimes planted in this way.

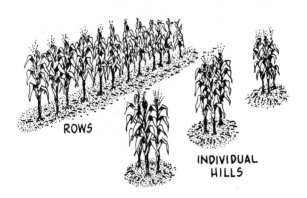

Usual method of planting is to sow 7 to 10 seeds in a 12 to 18-inch circle, and thin to the strongest 3 or 4 plants.

MOUND PLANTING

Squash and melons require lots of water, yet often suffer if water covers their crowns. They are

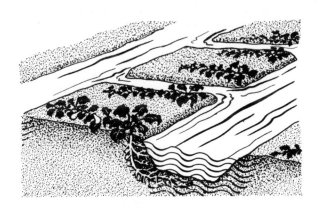

usually grown in mounds. Corn and tomatoes, too, can be grown in this manner.

MISCELLANEOUS "SYSTEMS"

Catch crops. Those vegetables which can be spotted almost anywhere in the vegetable or flower garden are sometimes referred to as "catch crops." Lettuce, onion sets, and radishes are three of the best examples, although beets can also be used if they are transplanted carefully. Use them to fill in blank spaces in rows of slower growing vegetables, mix them in the flower border, or plant them along the edge of a walk.

Interplanting: One way to get full production and maximum variety out of a small garden is to interplant quick-growing varieties between slower-

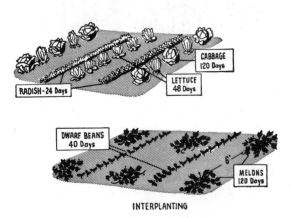

INTERPLANTING

growing ones, or to mix seeds of quick-maturing and slow-maturing varieties. Rows of fast crops—lettuce, radishes, mustard greens, kohlrabi, and bunching onions can be sandwiched in between slower-growing vegetables. Pole beans are often planted in hills with corn; the cornstalks take the place of poles.

In order to keep a wide variety of vegetables available for the table at all times, the home gardener should strive for a succession of fresh crops by continuous planting of small quantities of the same vegetable at frequent intervals.

Succession plantings: The normal succession of crops is from the cool-weather varieties such as peas and lettuce to the warm-weather vegetables of the bean and corn class to the cool fall varieties such as cabbage, cauliflower, collards, endive, or Chinese cabbage. It is wise to think ahead a season or two.

ROTATION

Because different crops affect soils in different ways and take different elements out of the soil, no one crop should be planted in the same place in the garden year after year. The root crops, for example, draw heavily upon the potash and phosphorus in the soil. They should be followed by peas or beans, or by one of the leaf crops, since they use those elements in smaller proportions.

how to include vegetables in your landscape plans

On these 8 pages you will find a potpourri of ideas for vegetable gardening in small space. Yet, it would be wrong to say that this chapter is only for people who have small gardens, for here you will also find some ways to use the ornamental qualities of many vegetables to advantage in *any* garden.

Once we saw a most interesting formal bedding of red and green foliage against a white wall. Scarlet runner beans were trained against the fence, a row of rhubarb chard came next, then two rows of dark red geraniums, and the whole finished off by a border of beets. This might have been even more effective if the planting had been done in clumps or drifts instead of rows. The point to remember is this: *Vegetables take on a more individual character if disassociated from their usual row planting.*

Here, then, are some observations and suggestions for those who only have a few square feet of garden and for those who have acreage galore but would just like to try something different with vegetables.

• Rhubarb makes an admirable tub plant. If well watered and fed, it stays handsome until frost. If the soil is well enriched with manure, it can remain in the tub for several years. Tub-grown rhubarb is easy to force; many cold-climate gardeners do it, simply by moving it to the basement in January and pulling stalks as they appear. Certainly this is much easier than the usual forcing method which involves digging the roots and packing them in sand.

• A bed of blue curled kale is almost as rich looking as a bed of ferns. Or use flowering kale; the inner leaves are marbled and veined with pink, chartreuse, cream, and rose.

• Plant cucumber vines or small summer squash atop a retaining wall, and allow them to trail over. The warmth of a cement wall, particularly, will induce unusually heavy fruiting.

• Parsley and lettuce make crisp, fresh-looking border edgings or can be grown in clumps among low-growing annuals or perennials. Try trimming a border of perky dwarf French marigolds with curly parsley. Frilled or cut-leafed lettuces such as Prizehead, Oak Leaf, and Black Seeded Simpson give a satisfying finish to borders of snapdragons or penstemons. Sow seed of lettuce in the open ground when you set out plants of the flowers. About the time flowers begin to set buds, the lettuce will be harvested.

• Treat red cabbage as the ornamental it is and plant it here and there in the flower border.

• As a lovely, feathery background, asparagus is worth growing even if you never cut a single spear.

• Among the "naturals" for raised beds and containers are: red rhubarb chard, crinkly red and green leaf lettuce, purple cabbage, green bell peppers, and purple eggplant.

• Try growing 2 or 3 cucumber vines or summer squash plants in a large wooden tub or box, 18 inches deep. They'll need the usual extra water and fertilizing that container plants demand, but they'll produce generously and make a conversation piece for your patio.

• In damp, partly shaded spots where most vegetables won't grow, plant parsley, chives, or mint. Sink a pot or can of mint under a garden faucet where it will catch the drips and an extra dose of water when you turn on the hose.

• Grow eggplant in an elevated place so that you can see the blossoms which turn down from under the purple-tinged leaves. Actually, the leaves are handsome in themselves. The fruit has an incomparable color. It is matchless in arrangements — try it with cucumbers, okra, and green pepper.

• Swiss chard is a real charmer when used as an edging along the front walk or along a garden path.

• Where you want a dramatic effect, no vegetable (and few other plants) can shunt aside that "delicious thistle" — the artichoke.

• Twelve kernels of hybrid corn planted in a sunny patio corner will produce a lush, tropical growth that looks like a cluster of young banana trees until the tassels form in late August.

Here is an ideal set-up for growing vegetables. Beds are a good width for easy care, and are raised slightly for drainage. Brick paths always remain dry, and take a wheelbarrow with room to spare. This idea could work equally well on a smaller scale. Design: Eckbo, Royston, and Williams.

SOME CARDINAL RULES FOR THE SMALL-SPACE GARDENER

1. Concentrate on vegetables that taste better when home grown than when market-purchased. Never mind the potatoes, the celery, the parsnips, the winter squash; go heavy on carrots, beets, beans, peas, tomatoes, asparagus — and at least a token planting of sweet corn.

2. Concentrate on crops that give high returns for space required. For instance, Swiss chard doesn't take much more space than spinach yet yields over a much longer period.

3. Start as many plants as possible in flats, so that the time they are in the ground is shortened.

4. Grow as many plants as possible vertically rather than horizontally. Use trellises and stakes for supporting vegetables such as tomatoes and cucumbers.

5. Grow vegetables in tubs and raised beds.

6. Don't be afraid to use boxes for lettuce, green onions, etc., even though boxes are shallow. Boxes 12 inches deep will grow beets, carrots, chard, and many other vegetables if close attention is given soil, moisture, and drainage through holes in the bottom.

7. Don't overlook the use of many vegetables as border plants in the vegetable garden.

8. Consider more than just the obvious locations. How about the fence corners, the back porch, the balcony or deck, the roof?

Open sections in a paved area can be attractive as well as practical. Paving helps to hold moisture, provides "insulation," and keeps out weeds.

space-saving ideas

FIFTEEN-BY-TWENTY-FOOT GARDEN

Take a good look at the figures on the margins of the vegetable garden plan below. Those aren't yards; they are *feet*. There are few gardens, indeed, that cannot accommodate a vegetable-raising area at least this size. Planted in the manner shown, or even with some variation, this 300 square feet can easily yield enough vegetables for a family of four.

Actually, the plan does not show all of the vegetables that might be grown in this space. Such crops as green onions and radishes are omitted, because it is assumed that they can be tucked into odd corners to fill space between corn and other widely-spaced plants.

The variations on this plan are endless. If, for example, your family dislikes beets, make it two rows of carrots. The artichokes and rhubarb, both perennial vegetables that take a couple of years before they begin to bear, might give way to more corn. If you are lukewarm about herbs along the path, this would be a handy spot for asparagus.

Notice that there are no potatoes or dry onions, both of which might as well be purchased because the factor of freshness and greenness is not involved. Others that have less general appeal, such as kale, leeks, parsnips, and turnips do not appear in this smaller plan. Note that vegetables are arranged so that tall types do not shade the low ones.

Dividing the vegetable garden into four sections in this manner facilitates rotation of crops in such a way that you can keep simple records of what you plant from season to season and year to year.

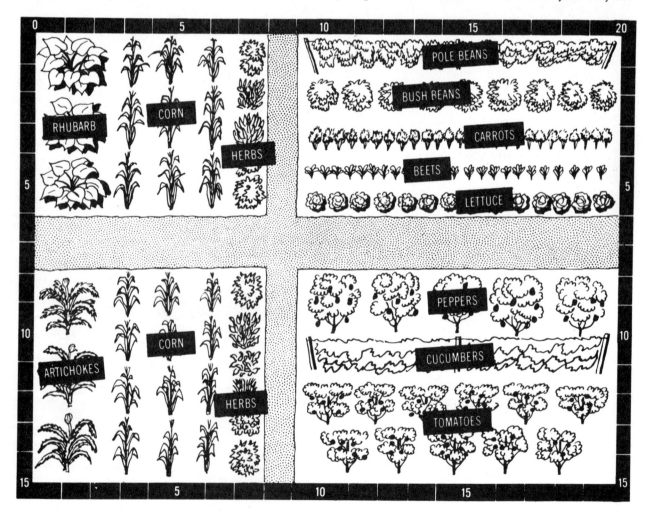

PLANT VEGETABLES WITH FLOWERS

Many gardeners who first grew vegetables and flowers together as an expediency in Victory garden days came to like the idea so well that they have done it ever since. Some vegetables just naturally respond to flower border treatment; others are so handsome in their own right that you look upon them as ornamentals and forget that they are called vegetables.

Leafy, frilly vegetables, such as lettuce and parsley, make beautiful edgings. Of the leaf lettuces, Prizehead, Oakleaf, Simpson, Salad Bowl, and Bibb are especially useful; if sown in a fairly broad swath, and thinned as they grow, they will provide an edging that is presentable for 2 or 3 months. If

planted behind a row of lobelia, dwarf ageratum, or fibrous begonias, you need not worry about bare spots that will appear as you harvest the lettuce.

Beets and carrots, whose leaves are as decorative as their roots are useful, respond to the extra watering they are likely to receive in a bed of flowers or near the lawn.

Red chard has long been accepted as an ornamental, both in the garden and in arrangements.

The first time we saw it was in a border where it had been planted in front of *Abelia floribunda*, a flowering shrub whose leaves have a definite bronze cast, especially in their young stages. Groups of tall white sweet william, which can pass as a perennial phlox from a distance, were interplanted with the chard, whose large, rich red leaves often have an orange mid-rib.

Rhubarb, itself, has most of the qualifications of a tropical plant, what with its large, glossy, deeply crinkled leaves on strong red stems. It is beautiful

in large borders, where it can be used to produce luxuriant tropical effects. As mentioned previously, it is handsome and distinctive in containers.

The artichoke might be considered a gray counterpart of the rhubarb. It is used as an ornamental by many gardeners and landscape architects, who have found that its soft gray-green leaves — like large fern fronds — are unduplicated in any shrub or perennial in the so-called purely ornamental class. Here

are effective uses for artichokes: as a hedge dividing a lawn from an orchard; on either side of a drive; in a large perennial border in front of massive groups of tall delphiniums.

Okra, especially the new ornamental Red River, makes an attractive flowering and fruiting hedge in warmer climates. "Dwarf Long Pod Green" is only 3 to 4 feet high; use it if your landscape calls for a short plant.

space-saving ideas

VEGETABLES IN RAISED BEDS

Raised beds offer certain unduplicated advantages to the home vegetable gardener. Watering and fertilizing are easily controlled; cultivating, weeding, and harvesting become more efficient and involve less backbending. More important, however, is the additional depth of soil provided through elevation above the existing ground level. In the case of heavy adobe or clay, you can superimpose a layer of good topsoil rather than struggle to improve the existing soil, a process that may take quite some time and require the addition of large quantities of sand, manure, and various soil conditioners. Because of the improved drainage and better aeration provided in raised beds, the soil does not become waterlogged in winter, and as a result, warms up faster in spring and produces earlier crops.

The simplest form of raised bed is that shown below. Rectangular in form, it is enclosed with 2-by 10-inch redwood boards reinforced at the corners. Although its length can be adjusted to fit the size of the garden, a 3-foot width, sufficient to accommodate 2 or 3 rows of smaller vegetables such as lettuce, carrots, or beets, is about the minimum for efficiency.

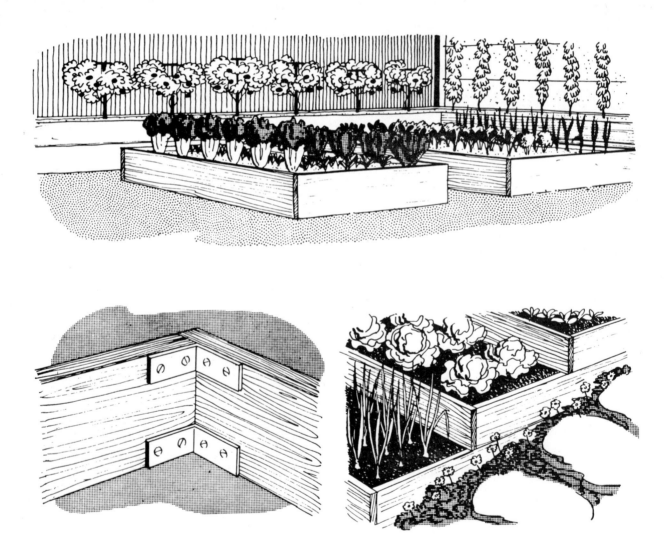

THREE-TIERED RAISED BED

Not only does the elevation of this unique example make it possible to grow 3 times as many vegetables as could be accommodated in a bed occupying the same amount of ground space, but the extra depth of soil, and the protection afforded by the wall at the back, provide unusually advantageous growing conditions.

The largest single item you'll need is soil, especially in the back section, which will be 30 or 36 inches high, depending on whether you use 10-inch or 12-inch lumber. The front and middle sections are raised 10 or 12 inches and 20 or 24 inches high respectively. Tie bolts secured to galvanized or aluminum wire prevent the boards from bulging from the weight of moist soil. After filling the bed to within an inch of the top, water several days before planting so soil will settle (probably about 2 inches).

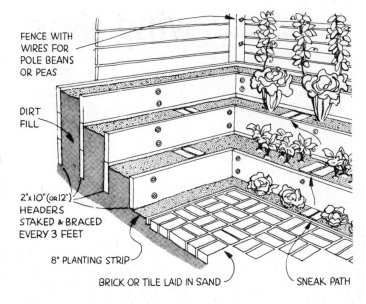

FENCE WITH WIRES FOR POLE BEANS OR PEAS

DIRT FILL

2"x10"(or 12") HEADERS STAKED & BRACED EVERY 3 FEET

8" PLANTING STRIP

BRICK OR TILE LAID IN SAND

SNEAK PATH

MODULAR CONTAINERS

These matched sets of plant boxes can be used effectively for either flowers or small vegetables. The 6-inch depth will be sufficient for green onions, radishes, many kinds of lettuce, spinach, parsley, chives, and shorter-rooted varieties of carrots. Herbs of all kinds will thrive in them. Your menu will never lack for crisp greens.

If arranged in patterns similar to those shown at the bottom of the illustration, these boxes can become a decorative part of a terrace or any other outdoor living area. They are small enough and light enough to be moved at will. Older gardeners find that sawbuck type platforms raise modular containers for easy access. Varying the height of platforms adds another dimension of interest.

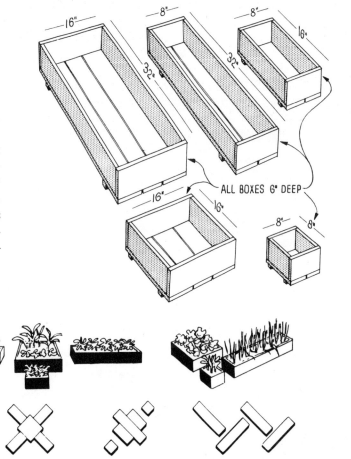

ALL BOXES 6" DEEP

space-saving ideas

DOORSTEP SALAD GARDEN

Even though you have an acre of vegetables, it still will pay you to grow a salad garden near your kitchen door. In a box, or in 2 or 3 tubs, you can keep a continuous succession of leaf lettuce, radishes, and green onions coming on. Small sowings every 3 or 4 weeks will furnish the makings of green salads most of the year. One of the beauties of the

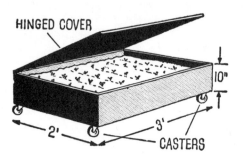

salad box is its availability and the ease with which it can be protected from birds, snails, and other hazards of the open garden. If you put your box on casters, it can be moved easily in or out of the sun.

RICHARD DAWSON

Red chard, lettuce, parsley are attractive in pots.

RAISED BED FOR ROOT VEGETABLES

Raised beds for root vegetables have special advantages besides their neat appearance. It's easier to fill a raised bed with the rich, light soil that root crops demand than it is to build up or to replace

S. C. WILSON

Carrots, other root vegetables thrive in raised bed.

dirt in a bed at ground level. Also, good drainage is assured, and tiny seedlings are kept safe from foot traffic.

Carrots make a thrifty crop for a raised bed; they can be planted close together to get the maximum yield from a small space. Radishes, green onions, and potatoes are other crops that do especially well in raised beds.

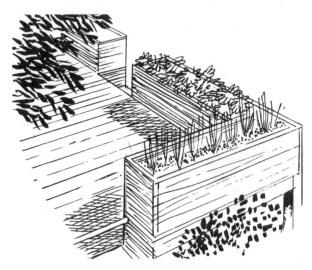

Raised beds are effective around the edge of a deck.

Herb box conveniently located near kitchen door contains parsley, rosemary, chives, mint, tarragon. The design is by Eckbo, Royston, and Williams.

Concrete blocks can be used as individual "raised beds" for border of herbs beside a garden walk. Concrete grille units are also effective.

YOU CAN GROW HERBS ALMOST ANYWHERE

Herbs are remarkably free-wheeling plants. Few people have space or need for a large collection of herbs, but there's always demand for an attractive and serviceable ground cover, an edging, a shrub, or a container plant. Herbs fill all these needs.

Perhaps the greatest opportunities for successful herb culture are in the realm of container gardening. Herbs have a happy way of thriving in boxes, planters, pots, and raised beds. Almost without exception these plants crave the sun and like a soil that drains readily and warms up quickly.

Even in colder climates, it should be possible to find a protected corner or a sunny wall for a planter or raised bed such as you see here. And, of course, many of these plants, being culinary herbs, should be grown as close to the house as possible, for ready use.

Among the herbs which make excellent subjects for containers and raised beds are: thyme, marjoram, sage, and savory.

Parsley, in addition to its kitchen uses for flavoring and garnishing, also makes a handsome edging or border plant. Here it is combined with spring bulbs.

In planter near front door, handsome dwarf rosemary offers fragrant welcome to visitors. Plant has dark green, needle-like leaves, blue flowers in winter.

artichokes

This bold, showy perennial adapts itself best to certain mild-climate areas of the West; it does particularly well in the fog belt along the California coast. While 3 or 4 plants will provide plenty of artichokes for a small family, a planting of a dozen or so along the back fence or the edge of the lawn will add variety and interest to any garden.

CHARACTERISTICS

Artichoke — like asparagus and rhubarb — is a perennial vegetable and a cool-season crop. A mature plant may reach 6 feet in height with long, gray-green, pinnately cut leaves. Home gardeners will find it most convenient to grow artichokes from nursery-purchased offshoots or divisions, rather than from seed. Once an artichoke has become established, it will remain vigorous and productive for 5 or 6 years.

Regional considerations: Artichokes are very sensitive to cold weather, and if you live in a section of the country where the ground freezes, it is impractical to grow them except as annuals, with a short harvest period in early fall. They like a climate where summers are comparatively cool, allowing bud growth to proceed slowly; they are at their best in the California coastal fog belt from Marin County south to Santa Barbara County.

Recommended variety: Green Globe.

PLANTING INSTRUCTIONS

When to plant: Plant divisions in late winter and early spring.

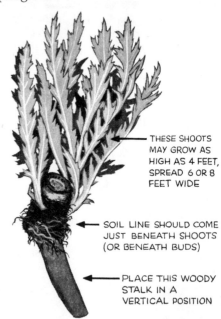

THESE SHOOTS MAY GROW AS HIGH AS 4 FEET, SPREAD 6 OR 8 FEET WIDE

SOIL LINE SHOULD COME JUST BENEATH SHOOTS (OR BENEATH BUDS)

PLACE THIS WOODY STALK IN A VERTICAL POSITION

How to plant: Place divisions in the soil with the old woody stalk in a vertical position and the base of the new leafy shoots just above the ground. Space them 3 to 4 feet apart in rows, leaving 4 to 5 feet between rows. Artichokes need a sunny location, but in hot summer areas they will do better with half-day shade. They like rich, loose, well-drained soil.

CULTURE

Hoe weeds as soon as you notice them; they steal much-needed water and nutrients from the plants. With generous watering, and a feeding with high-nitrogen fertilizer before buds form, plants will bear a few artichokes the first season. From the second year on, plants will yield 40 to 50 globular flower buds (edible parts of the plant) from early winter through early spring in the ideal growing conditions of California's fog belt. In most regions, however, buds will not be ready for picking until early summer.

Cut when buds are about 2 to 4 inches in diameter, but before the bracts start to separate or open. Each stalk carries a number of buds, but the top, or terminal, bud is always the biggest. Cut each bud with about 1½ inches of the stalk. After each stem has

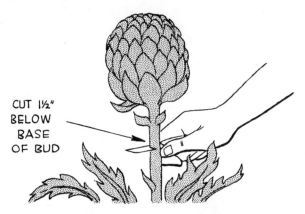

CUT 1½"
BELOW
BASE
OF BUD

given its last artichoke, it will seem to fold up, and the leaves will die back to a degree. This is the signal for you to cut that stem or stalk back to the base. New shoots, which grow from the base of the old stump, will develop their own fruiting stalks.

In mild-climate areas, apply fertilizer (artichokes like a fertilizer that is high in nitrogen) between the time you cut the last buds and the start of new growth. In cold-winter areas, cut back foliage in late November and cover the plant with the leaves plus 1 foot of some loose mulch such as straw. In spring, when all danger of frost is past, remove the mulch and feed the plants.

Artichokes are heavy feeders, and two or three additional fertilizer boosts during the growing season will help to promote vigorous growth.

INSECT PESTS

Aphids are almost universal pests on artichokes. Several types attack this vegetable. One species is found on the underside of the leaves. The artichoke buds can become infested with both green and black types.

It is generally unsafe to spray after buds have formed, because artichoke buds have an irregular surface with deep cavities from which spray residue is difficult to remove. If aphids cluster on the stems, just below the forming buds that you are going to eat, wash them off with a strong blast of water. Then there will be no question about insecticide residue when you serve artichokes at the dinner table.

Slugs and snails can cause serious damage to artichoke buds; to control them, set out bait at the base of each plant.

asparagus

Few gardeners realize that asparagus is one of the most permanent and dependable of the home garden vegetables. Although plants take 3 years to come into full production, they then reward you for waiting by providing a seasonal crop for many years afterward. Asparagus takes up space, but it does so in the grand manner; its tall, graceful growing habit makes it an ornamental favorite.

CHARACTERISTICS

Asparagus is a perennial and a cool-season crop that produces from March to June, well ahead of other vegetables. It is a tall grower — often fence-high — with many light branching stems; a long, narrow strip at the back of a lot is worth planting to asparagus even if ordinary vegetable gardening doesn't appeal to you. The home gardener will find that it pays to buy crowns for planting (growing this vegetable from seed is a slow proposition). One-year-

old asparagus crowns make the best plants because they suffer less in transplanting than older field-grown crowns. Avoid buying crowns that are wilted, moldy, or that have few roots. Plants will not reach full maturity for 3 years; once established, however, they will go on producing year after year—sometimes for 15 years or more.

Regional considerations: Can be successfully grown anywhere, with the exception of the southernmost regions of the Gulf states.

Recommended variety: Mary Washington.

PLANTING INSTRUCTIONS

When to plant: Early spring is best, although winter planting is quite common in mild-winter areas.

How to plant: Asparagus thrives best in deep, loose, fertile soil prepared about 2 weeks before you plant the crowns. You need roughly 200 square feet for an asparagus bed containing 2 rows about 20

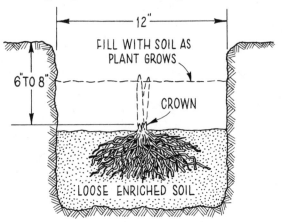

feet long set about 4 to 6 feet apart. This is a large enough space to accommodate between 30 and 40 plants, which is usually sufficient to supply a family of 4. Dig trenches 1 foot wide, 20 feet long, and 8 to 10 inches deep. Work from 3 to 6 inches of processed steer manure into about 6 inches of the soil in the bottom of the trench; then soak thoroughly. Set the asparagus crowns in the bottom of the trench so that the tops are between 6 and 8 inches below the top of the trench and the roots are spread out evenly. Space crowns about 12 inches apart and cover with 2 inches of loose, pulverized soil. Then water slowly and deeply.

CULTURE

As the young plants grow, fill in the trench little by little with loose soil, but don't cover the tips. By summer the trench will be completely filled. Water plants thoroughly every 7 to 10 days during the summer.

Because asparagus plants need at least 2 years to get established, you shouldn't harvest any spears the first year; rather, allow them to make foliage. When the foliage turns brown in late fall or early winter, cut the stems to the ground. Never cut foliage back too soon — it manufactures food for the roots for about 6 months following the harvest period.

In early March of the second year, you're ready to harvest your first asparagus crop. Cut spears for only 4 to 6 weeks, then allow the foliage to develop. From the third year on, you can harvest the crop for the full harvest period (8 to 10 weeks), or until spears become thin, indicating that food stored in the roots is about exhausted for the season.

Asparagus spears are ready to cut when they are about 6 to 8 inches long. However, some gardeners prefer the more delicate taste of spears only about 5 inches long. You can cut the spears at ground level, or a few inches below the soil, but you should not make any cuts closer than 2 inches from the crowns. To avoid possible injury to the crowns or to the new shoots that are developing below the ground, use an asparagus knife specially designed for the purpose.

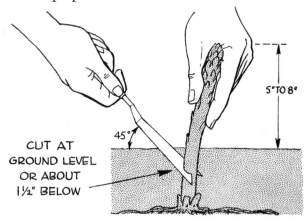

At the start of the cutting season, you will probably be able to harvest some spears every 3 days. As weather warms up and spears appear more rapidly, you may have to harvest the spears once or even twice a day. In cold-winter areas, mulch with well-rotted manure before the first frosts arrive to protect the root systems. Early each spring, cultivate and feed with a complete fertilizer.

INSECT PESTS

Asparagus beetle, cutworms, earwigs, snails, and slugs are the chief enemies of asparagus. Infestations of asparagus beetle on spears during cutting season can be brought under control by spraying or dusting with rotenone or malathion (*note label precautions*). A spray containing sevin may be applied to foliage *after* cutting season, for control of asparagus beetle, cutworms, and earwigs. Use bait to control snails and slugs.

beans

Beans are among the best of all crops for the home garden. They are rapid growers — 50 to 60 days from seed to maturity for most snap beans of the bush type; 60 to 90 days for snap pole beans and limas. The yield is great and the maintenance is low; probably the one time you'll have to give them much attention is at harvest time.

CHARACTERISTICS

There are beans and beans and beans — more kinds, varieties and strains than we could fully list and describe in an entire book of this size. Only two types, however, are grown by home gardeners to any extent: snap beans and lima beans. Each can be broken down into a low growing group (bush beans) and a tall growing group (pole beans). Bush beans are compact plants, growing 1 to 2 feet high depending on variety and growing conditions. Bush limas are attractive enough to serve as little hedges, in the vegetable garden or elsewhere. If you have a sunny planting area along a walkway that you generally plant to annuals, try a few bush limas this summer instead. The pole, or climbing beans take slightly longer to mature than bush beans, but once established they will outproduce the others by a wide margin.

Both snaps and limas are warm weather crops, and their culture is much the same. Before deciding which kind you prefer to grow, be reminded of this basic difference in the end product: unlike snap beans, lima beans must be shelled. What's more, the shelling is a slow and rather laborious process — much more so than in the case of peas, for instance. (Of course, a true lima-lover may scoff at this and even voice a preference to shelling limas over breaking the ends from snap beans.)

Regional considerations: Beans are grown in most sections of the United States. They do their best where summers are warm and where sun is plentiful; where cold summer fogs are common, beans should not be planted.

Recommended varieties: *Snap (bush):* Topcrop, Pencil Pod Wax, Burpee's Tender Pod, Tendercrop, Greencrop, Dwarf Horticultural. *Snap (pole):* Kentucky Wonder, Romano, Scarlet Runner, Oregon Giant, Stringless Blue Lake, Burpee Golden. *Lima (bush):* Fordhook (many strains available), Henderson, and for the Southeast, Jackson Wonder and Dixie Butterpea. *Lima (pole):* Florida Butter, King of the Garden, Sieva. There are many other varieties that do exceptionally well in certain areas or under certain conditions, and it is wise to check with a local nurseryman before deciding which seed you should use.

PLANTING INSTRUCTIONS

When to Plant: Plant first seeds after frosts are past and soil has warmed up. Successive plantings can be made through late spring and summer, up until about 8 weeks before first fall frosts are due.

How to Plant: Beans need a light, well drained soil if they are to germinate properly and penetrate the inch of soil that covers them. Seeds will rot if soil is wet or too cold. Plant seeds of bush types 1 inch deep, 3 inches apart in rows, with 2 to 3 feet between rows. Rather than planting all at once, plant several 20-foot rows — one at a time — at 2-week intervals, beginning early in the planting season with the last planting about 60 days before frost is due. This will assure a continuous supply.

Teepees are the easiest support to make for pole beans. Take three or four poles and plunge them 6 inches deep. Lean them in and tie together where they meet. Sow 2 or 3 seeds at the base of each pole. Beans can also be sown along a wall, fence, or trellis, and trained on wire or heavy twine.

8' SINGLE POLE

3 POLES

CULTURE

Beans — like most vegetables — must be watered regularly and not allowed to dry out. Particularly in the case of the pole types, there is a tremendous leaf and stem area to be supplied — to say nothing of the beans themselves. A slow-soak method is preferable to overhead watering, which may lead to mildew.

Beans respond well to feedings with commercial fertilizer; well-fed bush beans yield 4 to 6 pickings, pole types 6 to 10. To avoid "burning" seeds or young seedlings, hold off on the fertilizer until plants are well on their way. A second feeding, just as the pods start to form, is also beneficial.

Both snaps and limas should be picked every 4 to 7 days, while they are quite young. Pods that are allowed to mature not only result in poor edibility, but also cause weakened plants and shorter harvesting seasons. Pick beans with care, so as not to injure the vines.

INSECT PESTS

Mexican bean beetle is a common pest in most states east of the Rocky Mountains. Adults and larvae feed on pods and also undersides of leaves. Control with rotenone, malathion, or methoxychlor.

Aphids (usually black) are also pests of beans. Control them with rotenone or malathion. If diabrotica (spotted cucumber beetle) attacks, dust or spray with sevin. Whiteflies, the nymphs of which feed on the underside of leaves, can be controlled with several contact sprays. Malathion, diazinon, or sevin are particularly effective.

As is true with all vegetable spraying, be sure to follow precautions on the label so that you will not spray too close to the harvest date.

Beets are a thoroughly satisfying crop. Their needs are few, they grow rapidly from seed, and they are delicious whether cooked or eaten raw (the greens are good, too). They are disease-free, and insects seldom give them a second glance. Primarily for these reasons, they stand high in the upper rank as a favorite of home gardeners everywhere.

CHARACTERISTICS

Beets, along with two of the other root crops — carrots and turnips — are exceedingly easy to grow. Seed, sown right where plants are to grow, reach full maturity in 55-80 days (most varieties take about 60 days). They are at their best when grown fast and eaten young. They will grown in almost any kind of soil, but perform best in soils which are neither too light nor too heavy.

Regional considerations: Hardy and easily adaptable; they can be grown anywhere.

Recommended varieties: Detroit Dark Red, Early Wonder, Ruby Queen.

PLANTING INSTRUCTIONS

When to plant: Most important thing to remember when planting beets is that they do not grow well in hot weather, and therefore, should not be planted in summer or even late spring in hot-summer regions. In cold-winter regions, the usual planting time is just as early in spring as ground can be worked, and for about a month thereafter. In many parts of the South, beets are planted in late fall and winter. In the coastal regions of Southern California, many home gardeners grow beets. successfully 12 months of the year.

How to plant: Sow seeds ½ inch deep, in soil that will not crust. If you have a light soil that dries out rapidly, soak seeds before planting to facilitate rapid germination.

The most common error is to have too many beets ripening at one time. Best results can be obtained by planting a 10-foot row every week or two throughout the growing season. Each row will yield about 50 delicious, tender, small beets.

CULTURE

Thin seedlings to 2 or 3 inches apart when they have grown to about 6 inches high. It is possible to transplant extra seedlings with a fair degree of success. Be sure the small root is planted straight down. Also, as with other transplanting, do the job in the evening or in overcast weather so roots can have time to get at least partially set before the sun starts drawing moisture from the leaves.

Overhead sprinklings with a light, mist-like spray, of long enough duration to soak the ground 6 inches or more, will keep plants growing without interruption and at the same time keep both tops and roots fresh and crisp. Until the tops grow large enough to cover the spaces between rows, it is well to follow up watering with a light surface cultivation to prevent the formation of cracks in the soil.

After plants have been thinned, apply a commercial fertilizer to insure rapid and uninterrupted growth.

Many vegetable enthusiasts value beets mainly for their tops, which are both tasty and nutritious (boil or steam them like spinach, or serve in salads). Young thinned plants will give you a good supply. To keep beet greens coming along throughout the year, try broadcasting seed in small areas in a corner of the vegetable garden, here and there in the flower border, or as a decorative border on the terrace. If you have room in the lathhouse, sow a flat of seeds; bring them along in the flat until they are 3 or 4 inches tall, and harvest in one sweep for greens.

INSECT PESTS

Beets are one of the most pest-free and disease-free of all vegetables. Snails and slugs will often eat young seedlings; put out baits early to prevent injury.

broccoli

Best all-around member of the cole crops (cabbage family) for home gardens is broccoli. It is hardy, relatively easy to grow, and can be harvested over a long period. Buy started plants from nurseries, and time your planting so the growing season is during cool months.

CHARACTERISTICS

A cool-season grower, similar to cauliflower in some ways, but hardier and easier to grow. Grows to 4 feet in height, and has a branching habit.

This one is very sensitive to heat, especially heat combined with good growing conditions. At first you think it's growing mightily (which it is), but too suddenly you find that the heat has forced it to flower and it is past the good-eating stage.

It takes broccoli as long as 5 months to mature from seed, but only 60 to 80 days if set out as young plants. Because of this, and also because it takes only a dozen or so plants to keep plenty of broccoli on the family dinner plates, most home gardeners prefer to purchase small plants from a nursery for a few cents each.

Broccoli is valued for its green flower heads, largest of which is the initial (central) head which may be up to 6 inches in diameter. Once it has been cut, smaller shoots will continue to develop into heads for as long as 2 or 3 months, if fully formed heads are kept cut.

Cauliflower-broccoli differs from the sprouting type described above and is discussed in the cauliflower section of this book.

Regional considerations: Grown throughout the United States.

Recommended varieties: Green Sprouting (many strains available), DeRapa or Raab.

PLANTING INSTRUCTIONS

When to plant: In cold-winter areas, set out young plants in early spring, beginning about 2 weeks before average date of last frost. Plant again in midsummer for fall harvest. In mild-winter areas, plant broccoli from early fall through late winter.

How to plant: Space young plants 18 to 24 inches apart in rows, and leave 36 inches between rows. Soil should be very fertile, non-acid, and well drained.

CULTURE

There are few special cultural techniques for the home gardener to remember. As is the case with most vegetables a systematic watering program is essential. Broccoli will thrive if fed with commercial fertilizer once or twice during the growing season, before heads begin to form.

Harvesting just at the right time is very important if broccoli is to be at its edible best. Cut the heads while they are hard and green; never wait until the clustered buds begin to crack. When cutting, include 5 or 6 inches of the edible portion of the stem and leaves.

INSECT PESTS

You will have to keep your eyes open for the same pests that attack cabbage. The two most common pests in home gardens are cabbageworm and aphids, both of which can be controlled with malathion.

Brussels sprouts

The oft-used nickname "thousand-headed cabbage" is a bit on the flattering side; nevertheless, a single plant will reproduce up to a hundred delectable sprouts, some of them the size of golf balls. Brussels sprouts aren't as commonly grown as some other vegetables, but if you live in a cool, moist climate where summers don't sizzle you will find this vegetable to be easy and fun to grow.

CHARACTERISTICS

Don't ever drop the final "s" in Brussels, because this vegetable is actually named for the capital of Belgium where it has been grown for hundreds of years. Brussels sprouts are a member of the cabbage family, and — appropriately enough — the sprouts themselves look like tiny cabbages. It takes about 4 months for a planted seed to reach full maturity. The plants are erect and rather unusual in appearance, particularly when the sprouts (buds) are ready to be picked. By this time, excess leaves should have been removed from all but the topmost part of the plant (these continue to nourish the plant) to make room for the ever-crowding sprouts growing from the leaves' axils. The plant, from the ground up, is one big cluster of tiny "cabbages" except for these upper leaves.

Regional considerations: Can be grown in many sections of the U. S., but is not commonly grown in some parts of the South. Brussels sprouts are a cool-weather crop and do exceptionally well in moist climates. Grown commercially in such widely separated areas as Long Island, New York, and the Northern California coastal regions south of San Francisco. Don't plant Brussels sprouts if you live in an area where summers are hot, long, and dry.

Recommended varieties: Long Island Improved, Catskill, Jade Cross Hybrid.

PLANTING INSTRUCTIONS

When to plant: Set out young plants in June and July so that plants will be mature and ready to pick in the fall. In mild climate areas, plant again in fall and winter.

How to plant: Set the young plants in fertile soil and in a sunny location, 18 inches apart in rows with 30 inches between rows. If you prefer to start from seed, plant them ¼ inch deep in flats about 4 to 6 weeks ahead of the time you intend to set them out. If you only want 10 or 12 plants, use compressed peat pots (see page 11).

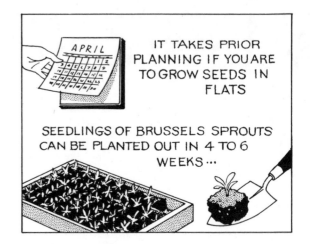

IT TAKES PRIOR PLANNING IF YOU ARE TO GROW SEEDS IN FLATS

SEEDLINGS OF BRUSSELS SPROUTS CAN BE PLANTED OUT IN 4 TO 6 WEEKS...

CULTURE

Planting methods and cultural requirements are practically identical to those of cabbage and cauliflower. Make absolutely certain that plants get plenty of water during the growing season.

Harvest the buds before they change color, taking the lowest sprouts on the stalk first. Plants may be harvested a little at a time over a period of 6 to 8 weeks, with one plant producing 75 to 100 sprouts. Firming the soil around the plant is said to encourage formation of sprouts and retard leaf growth.

Frost won't harm this hardy vegetable — it actually thrives and does its best in cold weather. In areas where there are winter snows, plants that are still bearing can simply be moved to any cool sheltered area such as the garage, and their roots buried in some soil. In this way, fresh Brussels sprouts may be picked for the dinner table until midwinter.

INSECT PESTS

Same as for cabbages.

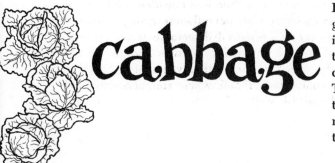

cabbage

If you only have a small amount of space in which to grow vegetables, then cabbage is not for you. However, if you have a generous-sized section of garden that seems to be just yearning for something to do, you will find cabbage to be a generous fall and winter producer. These round vegetables can also be showpieces — both the green and red leafed kinds. Try one of the purplish-red varieties in a small soy tub for a unique patio container plant.

CHARACTERISTICS

The best reasons for not planting cabbage are these: It takes up considerable garden space; it is attacked by more than the usual number of pests and diseases; it has a long growing season and demands generous feedings during that season.

Reasons in favor of planting: High vitamin value of all varieties when eaten raw; it produces in great abundance during the fall and winter months; it is very hardy, withstanding short periods of temperatures as low as 10° to 15° below freezing.

There are many members of the cabbage family (also known as the cole crops). Some of these "cousins" — broccoli, Brussels sprouts, cauliflower, Chinese cabbage, collards, kale, and kohlrabi — are unique enough in their end product to merit separate discussion on these pages; their cultural requirements prior to harvest time, however, are pretty much the same as cabbage. Cabbage itself can be divided into many varieties and hybrids, but the main considerations are whether you wish to grow the regular green cabbage or red cabbage, and whether you prefer early or late varieties or a combination of both.

It takes time and patience to grow cabbage from seed — early varieties take 90 to 125 days, late varieties 125 to 150 days. For this reason, and because cabbage takes up considerable space, most home gardeners prefer to purchase just a few young plants from a nursery.

Fast growing vegetables such as radishes and early lettuce can be planted between young cabbage plants and harvested before cabbage starts to spread out and take up space.

Regional considerations: Grows well in all sections of the U.S., although best times to plant vary according to region (see planting instructions, below).

Recommended varieties: *Early, small heads:* Copenhagen Market, Badger Market, Emerald Cross, Early Jersey Wakefield. *Early, medium size heads:* Golden Acre, Marion Market, Red Acre (purplish red), Globe, King Cole Hybrid. *Late, very large heads:* Danish Ballhead, Burpee's Surehead, Mammoth Red Rock (purplish red). *Savoy varieties* (milder, more delicate flavor than regular cabbage): Savoy King, Chieftain.

PLANTING INSTRUCTIONS

When to plant: Time plantings so maturity will be reached before or after the hot summer months. In cold-winter areas, set out plants as early as possible in the spring, so heads will form no later than early summer. For cabbages in late fall and early winter, young plants should be set out in midsummer (or in early fall where summers are hot).

How to plant: Set out young plants 12 to 18 inches apart in rows (early varieties) or 18 to 30 inches apart (late varieties), with about 30 inches between rows. Plants like a sunny location. Soil should be rich and fertile, and non-acid. It is important to plant cabbages firmer and deeper than most vegetables since they form large, heavy heads and are apt to be blown over in strong winds or may lean after the ground is water-soaked. If you prefer to start your own seed, plant them ½ inch deep in flats. It will be 6 to 8 weeks before plants are ready to be set out.

So that all your cabbages won't ripen at the same time, plant several every week or two, or plant a combination of early and late varieties.

CULTURE

A steady and uniform supply of moisture is imperative for all cabbage crops, and any check in their growth followed by a resumption of growth results in cracking of the cabbage heads. Select yellows-resistant varieties wherever this disease has been prevalent.

The extremely large leaf area of cabbages makes

it possible for them to use not only generous amounts of moisture, but also of fertilizers, particularly those high in nitrogen and phosphates. The first feeding should take place as soon as the plants are established, with successive feedings every 3 or 4 weeks thereafter until the heads begin to form. Ureaform nitrogen releases slowly, lessening chances of heads splitting from a sudden spurt in growth. Avoid very heavy applications of plant food.

As plants grow, mound soil around the stems to support tops. Additional roots will grow from the covered stems. Pick cabbages when heads are firm.

INSECT PESTS

Aphids, if not the most serious pest to cabbages in home gardens, are probably the most prevalent and persistent. Control them with rotenone or malathion (*note label precautions*).

The most serious pest of the cabbage is the green cabbageworm, the larva of a small white butterfly often found hovering over the cabbage patches in late spring. Cabbageworm feeds on undersides of leaves, producing ragged holes, and often burrows into the heads. Good control can be achieved by using one of the dusts or sprays for chewing insects; rotenone, diazinon, and sevin are the most effective.

Cabbage root maggot, a small yellowish-white maggot which tunnels into the roots and causes plants to wilt, can be controlled by spraying ground around young seedlings with diazinon.

carrots

Of all the root crops, carrots are year-in-and-year-out the people's choice. Give them a sandy or loamy soil and a place in the sun and they will grow anywhere in the United States. Seed is rather slow and difficult to germinate, but if you know this in advance (and now you do) you can take simple precautions to solve the problem.

CHARACTERISTICS

The carrot, king among root crops, is a hardy plant — one of the best cool-season growers. There are varieties suited to various types of soils, and no garden need be without a supply of carrots.

Like other root crops, carrots should be grown from seed directly in the ground. Most varieties take between 65 and 75 days from seed to full maturity.

Regional considerations: Carrots are one of the most popular vegetables in home gardens everywhere.

Recommended varieties: Starting with the longest and working down to the shortest, here are but a few of the many outstanding carrot varieties for home gardens. Length in inches is indicated in parentheses after each variety. Tendersweet (8½-10), Gold Pak (8½-10), Imperator (8), Danvers Half Long (7), Touchon (7), Nantes (6), Red Cored or Royal Chantenay (5½), Oxheart (4½), French Forcing (2). The new variety, Waltham Hi-Color (8½ to 10 inches) is resistant to a leaf blight that is serious in the Southeast.

PLANTING INSTRUCTIONS

When to plant: Spring and fall are the two best times to plant seed. Unlike other root crops, carrots can also be grown in summer with a fair degree of success except where extremely hot summers bake the soil hard and dry.

How to plant: Plant seeds ½ inch deep in a light or medium soil, in a sunny location. Soil should be free of clods and rocks, and should contain no fresh manure; any of these conditions can cause split roots. If you have a heavy soil, conditioning only the top 3 or 4 inches will do you no good; the carrots will grow straight down until they hit the "road block" or unworked soil, and then do a 90° turn.

Sow more seeds than you need — about 30 for each foot of row — to allow for a certain amount of non-germination. Leave 12 inches between rows.

Due to the long period it takes carrot seed to germinate (2 to 3 weeks), soaking the seed or mixing it with moist sand prior to sowing helps to speed germination and maintain moisture.

Carrot seeds must be fresh. They lose their germinating power more quickly than most seeds. Since the seed is small, hard, and dry, it rapidly loses the moisture given it at seed-sowing time. Therefore, the soil in contact with the seed must be kept moist at all times throughout the germinating period.

CULTURE

Most failures to get carrots started occur in warm weather. It is difficult to keep the seeded soil moist and crustless while seed is germinating. In small plantings a plastic sheet will do the trick. Remove as soon as the seedlings break through. A half-inch mulch of leaf mold or pulverized, rotted manure applied over the row after sowing will help to retain moisture. If the air is extremely hot and the seed

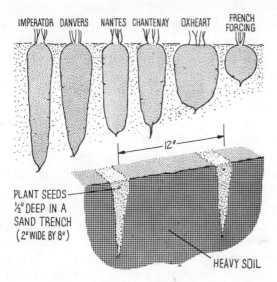

If your soil is heavy, condition the top few inches and grow one of the short varieties. Or try the sand trench method and grow whatever kinds you wish; just be sure to cover the row with burlap or black plastic so germinating seeds will stay moist in the sand. Feeder roots will grow sideways through sand and draw nutrients from the soil.

bed starts to dry out, water, applied with a fine spray, will seep through the mulch and moisten the seeded soil without disturbing it.

Fast growth is an essential for tender, juicy carrots. To achieve this result, provide a light, rich soil, side dressings with a commercial fertilizer, and plenty of water. Another benefit of rapid growth is the fact that the carrots reach maturity before being attacked by the carrot rust fly, a serious pest in some sections, especially during warm weather.

When tops show above ground, thin them to an inch apart. About 3 or 4 weeks later, when baby carrots have formed, thin again to 3 inches apart. These thinnings, ½ to 1 inch in diameter at the crown and about the size of your little finger, are a real gourmet item — their sweet flavor and tender texture is an "extra" known only to home vegetable gardeners.

Few home gardeners bother to freeze carrots, since they can easily be stored for several months. Cut off all but an inch or so of the tops and store in a cool, moist place.

INSECT PESTS

Carrot rust fly is the one enemy which can be considered serious. Its larva attacks the carrot underground, tunneling into the root. It is most prevalent in the Northeastern states and the coastal areas of the Pacific Northwest. Growing plants to maturity as rapidly as possible is an excellent preventive measure. Cool-season planting is another recommended control.

cauliflower

If you are willing to follow the cultural rules that apply to cabbage, *and then some*, you should plant cauliflower; otherwise, better stick to broccoli or one of the other cole crops. Perhaps the real answer as to whether to try this crop depends simply on how much you like the taste of super-fresh cauliflower!

CHARACTERISTICS

Growing good cauliflower takes some doing, but more than anything else, perhaps, it takes "a little bit o' luck." One ill-timed hot day, coupled with a failure to sprinkle on that day, can undo weeks or even months of patient work. On the other hand, if

growing conditions are good, the plants may grow to maturity with a minimum of attention.

In addition to regular cauliflower, there is also a cauliflower-type of broccoli that does quite well in the mild-winter sections of the West. It is grown and harvested in much the same manner as broccoli, and makes an excellent substitute for cauliflower.

Regional considerations: Can be grown in many regions of the U.S., but in areas where spring weather gets quite warm it should be grown as a fall crop. In warm sections of California and in other mild-winter areas, cauliflower is a good fall and winter crop.

Recommended varieties: Snowball is an outstanding early variety, available in a number of strains; most of them take between 52 and 65 days from the time young plants are set out. Purple Head takes about a month longer to mature; because of its color, there is no need for blanching.

PLANTING INSTRUCTIONS

When to plant: When you plant cauliflower depends on where you live — more so than with most other vegetables. If you live in an area where spring weather is quite cool, you can set out plants in late winter or early spring. In most areas of the country, it is safest for home gardeners to grow cauliflower as a fall crop, setting out young plants in late summer.

If you only wish to grow a few heads of cauliflower, you will save yourself time and trouble by purchasing a few young plants from a nursery. Raising your own plants from seed in flats is not difficult, but it takes time — (6 to 8 weeks).

How to plant: Make rows 3 feet apart. Space plants 2½ to 3 feet apart. Dig holes and fill with water or fertilizer starter solution. After it has soaked in, set transplants in holes so that soil level comes just below the lower petioles. Gently firm soil around base of plant.

Plant a few at frequent intervals to stretch the harvest.

If you grow your own plants from seed, sow them ¼ to ½ inch deep.

CULTURE

Follow the same procedures as with cabbage, keeping in mind that cauliflower is not as hardy as cabbage and is even more sensitive to hot, dry weather. If weather does get hot, sprinkle daily with a fine spray to create a little moisture and humidity. Don't let this sprinkling serve as a substitute for deep soaking, however; this technique is meant only to *augment* the regular watering program.

As the cauliflower head starts to form, toward the end of the growing period, pull the outer leaves over it and fasten with a string. This gives protection from the sun and helps the head ·to blanch properly. Some gardeners use strings of different colors to denote time of tying up.

The head or "curd" is ready to cut when the separate sections begin to separate and are easily distinguishable.

Cauliflower takes up considerable space, and intercropping between rows of cauliflower or even between the plants themselves is practically a "must" in the average home garden. Lettuce, radishes, or onion sets can be sown at the time you plant cauliflower. When these are ready for use, seeds of bush beans or peas can go in near the earlier-sown crops. Before these are ready to harvest, the cauliflower will be harvested and out of the way.

INSECT PESTS

The same insects that attack cabbage and broccoli will attack cauliflower, and controls are the same. Get set to control cabbageworms and aphids, particularly.

celery

By no stretch of the imagination can celery be considered an easy plant to grow, and yet it is really not as difficult as it is cracked up to be. It is a heavy feeder and a heavy drinker. It will only do well if the soil is exceptionally rich. It only grows well in cool weather, and will not tolerate temperature extremes. If you can meet these basic requirements, chances are you can grow excellent celery.

CHARACTERISTICS

Celery grows best in natural muck land, a type of soil that is exceedingly rich in organic matter. You can approximate this type in a home garden by working in large amounts of humus (well-rotted manure or processed steer manure is excellent).

Only the patient gardener should grow celery; it takes between 4 and 5 months to reach full maturity from seed, or about 3 months from small plants.

The two main types of celery are green celery and self-blanching (golden) celery. Of the two, green celery is easiest for the home gardener to grow.

Celeriac, a close relative of celery, has an enlarged root crown that is delicious when cut up and boiled or served in salads (do not eat the stalks and leaves). It is grown in the same manner as celery.

Regional considerations: Can be grown in most sections of the U.S. It is best suited to a climate where days are warm and sunny but nights are cool.

Recommended varieties: Golden Self Blanching (early), Burpee's Fordhook, Pascal, Utah.

PLANTING INSTRUCTIONS

When to plant: Celery is most frequently planted in early spring. Planting time depends mainly on climate, however. In areas where winters are mild, celery is best grown as a winter crop; where the fall season is long and cool, young plants can be set out in late summer. Spring-planted celery must not be set out until danger of frost is past. A few very cold nights will trigger "bolting," or flowering.

How to plant: Seed should be started in flats or in pots indoors (plant them $\frac{1}{16}$ inch deep) since germination is slow and 8 weeks or more are required to bring the seedlings up to planting-out size — that is, 3 or 4 inches high. (If you want only a few plants, you can save time by purchasing them from a nursery.) Plant the seedlings in double rows, about 8 inches apart in the row, 24 inches between rows.

For a successful crop you should add commercial fertilizer and a large amount of well-rotted manure to your soil, dug in under the row 12 inches deep.

CULTURE

Water is the number-one requirement of celery, once it has been planted out and started on the slow but steady road to maturity. Soak the ground around plants thoroughly and often. Every two or three weeks, apply a liquid fertilizer simultaneously with one of your watering sessions.

Work up some soil around the plants as they grow. This not only will help plants to grow upright, but also will result in a certain amount of blanching (whitening) of the stalk. Be careful not to get dirt into the center of the stalk.

Some gardeners blanch celery for a week or so before harvesting (even the self-blanching kinds) by blocking off sun with plant collars or boards. This is an extra that hardly seems worth the trouble, since the difference in flavor that results is very subtle and not necessarily an improvement.

There is no need to wait for full maturity before harvesting celery. Gardeners frequently harvest several of the younger stalks when plants are still 3 or 4 weeks away from full growth.

Celery stores well if dug up and kept with roots in soil in a cool place. Many gardeners leave fall surpluses in the soil during early winter, piling dirt and straw around them to protect against freezing and pulling the stalks as needed.

INSECT AND MICROBE PESTS

A number of pests are drawn to celery. Celery leaf tier, wireworms, and vegetable weevil can be controlled with sevin dust or spray when plants are young.

Control infestations of aphids with rotenone or malathion. Don't use malathion within 2 weeks of harvest. Use captan or maneb sprays to control leaf blights and mildew.

chard

Swiss chard is perhaps the most useful and in every way satisfactory vegetable for the home garden. It can be grown any month of the year in all but the coldest sections, and a single planting can be harvested for months. It makes an excellent spinach substitute, and is cooked in the same way; in fact, the only big difference between the two is that chard is much easier to grow.

CHARACTERISTICS

Chard is a member of the beet family, but differs in that it does not have a bulbous, enlarged root. It takes only 60 days from seed to maturity, and is valued as a leaf crop; the large, green, crinkly leaves with white stalks and mid-ribs can be cut from the plants as they grow. Leaves may be boiled like spinach, used in salads, or included in sandwiches as an occasional variation from lettuce. In addition to being good to eat, crimson rhubarb chard is highly ornamental in the garden or in cut arrangements.

Regional considerations: Chard is a hardy plant that can be grown anywhere in the U.S. One of chard's greatest virtues is its ability to withstand summer temperatures. Where spinach bolts to seed, Swiss chard goes right on producing.

Recommended varieties: Fordhook Giant, Rhubarb Chard, Lucullus, or Large Ribbed Dark Green.

PLANTING INSTRUCTIONS

When to plant: In cold-winter areas, sow seed in early spring and no later than June. In mild climates, seed can be sown any time of the year.

How to plant: Sow seeds ½ inch deep in any good fertile soil, in a sunny location. Leave 18 to 24 inches between rows. Thin plants to stand 12 inches apart in the rows. Use thinnings for greens or transplant them to extend the crop.

CULTURE

Growing procedure is much the same as for beets. The only possible way to fail in growing chard is to neglect watering, or allow it to become coarse and woody before picking. If outer leaves are cut regularly, chard will serve as a "cut-and-come-again" vegetable for many months.

INSECT PESTS

Chard is generally free of disease, and insect pests are of little consequence. Occasional infestations of aphids are easily controlled by a spraying or dusting with rotenone or malathion (*note label precautions*). On smooth-leafed types, blast aphids off with a jet of water from the hose.

chinese cabbage

Chinese cabbage gives you a mild flavor of cabbage, an even more handsome form than Romaine lettuce, and the usefulness of both. It is not as slow-growing as most of the cabbage crops and is one of the most decorative, especially after being picked and having had its outer leaves removed. As a salad green it has few equals.

CHARACTERISTICS

Chinese cabbage is definitely a cool-season crop. Unless you plant it early enough to mature crops before warm weather, or unless you plant it as a fall crop, it bolts to flower and seed before the heads have a chance to form.

Regional considerations: Grows well in all sections of the U.S.

Recommended varieties: Burpee Hybrid, Michihli. (Heads of the latter are nearly 20 inches high.)

PLANTING INSTRUCTIONS

When to plant: Treat it as your earliest spring and earliest fall planting.

How to plant: Plant seeds ½ inch deep as soon as soil can be worked in spring, or in late summer. Later, thin to 12 inches apart; if you thin while plants are quite small, surplus seedlings can be transplanted.

CULTURE

Chinese cabbage must be grown rapidly. In some ways its culture resembles lettuce more than cabbage, although it needs the same rich soil as all cabbage crops. Keep it coming on without check with plenty of water, and fertilize every 5 or 6 weeks.

The heads are ready to cut when they are firm and fully developed. Cut them close to the ground and remove the loose outside leaves.

INSECT PESTS

Chinese cabbage is generally free from attack. If aphids appear, dust or spray with malathion (*note label precautions*). Cutworms occasionally attack Chinese cabbage, particularly when plants are young. They come out of the ground at night to do their damage; there are a number of baits on the market which can be used to control cutworms.

collards

Collards, also called tree cabbage, have been hidden all too long in the South, where they are often grown in place of cabbage. Actually, they are adapted to a large growing area. These "headless cabbages" are prized for their delicious greens—leaves picked from the loose, non-heading types.

CHARACTERISTICS

Collards resemble a number of vegetables in different ways: They look much like cabbage, but do not form a head; they look somewhat like kale, but are taller growing (leaves are smooth and dark blue-green); you harvest them like chard, on a "cut-and-come-again" basis.

Regional considerations: Collards withstand more heat or cold than cabbage. While grown all over the U.S., they are more popular in the South and mid-South. Collards are planted in midsummer for fall and winter harvest in the South. Where summers are cool, they are spring-planted. Flavor improves after light frosts, becoming very sweet.

Recommended varieties: Georgia or Creole, Vates, Cabbage.

PLANTING INSTRUCTIONS

When to plant: Early spring and early summer. In the South, seed is sown from July through September for fall and winter harvest.

How to plant: Collards are very easy to grow from seed. Plant seeds ½ inch deep directly in the ground. Plants should stand 12 to 18 inches apart in rows 2 feet apart. Use thinnings as greens.

CULTURE

Despite their endurance of heat, collards must have an ample supply of soil moisture. Give them overhead sprinkling when possible.

Seeds grow to mature plants in about 75 days.

INSECT PESTS

Same as for cabbage.

corn

Corn likes heat. It should be planted after the ground has warmed up. Continue with small plantings every two weeks until midsummer. In estimating the amount to plant, figure 2 good ears to the stalk. Now, with these facts in mind, ask yourself: "How large a piece of property do I have, and what's the climate like?" The answer should help you to determine whether or not corn is for you.

CHARACTERISTICS

How many times, while out auto-exploring, have you passed a field of growing vegetables and wondered what they were? Chances are you never had to wonder if it happened to be *corn* growing out there. You knew it at a glance. And for this reason, let's forget about the descriptive phrases this time and get on with the how-to-do-it!

Regional considerations: Most of the nation's corn is grown in the Middle West, but home gardeners also grow this immensely popular vegetable in almost every section of the country. Even in cool-summer-climate areas of the Pacific Northwest, a gardener can grow excellent corn if he uses seed of a suitable early hybrid variety.

Recommended varieties: *Yellow:* Golden Bantam, Golden Cross Bantam, Iochief, Marcross, Carmelcross, Seneca Chief, Golden Beauty, F-M Cross, Illinichief Super Sweet, North Star. *White:* Country Gentleman, Silver Queen, Stowell's Evergreen Hybrid. The list we give here is only a partial list of proven favorites. What variety you should choose depends to a great extent on your soil and climate and when you plan to plant. Ask the advice of your nurseryman before you make your selection.)

PLANTING INSTRUCTIONS

When to plant: Plant first seeds two weeks after the average date of last frost, when soil has warmed, and follow with 3 or 4 more plantings at 2-week intervals so that the corn won't all ripen at once. Or buy early, midseason, and late varieties, plant some of each, and then do this all over again in about 3 weeks. (Corn seed matures in 75 to 90 days, depending on variety.)

How to plant: Plant seeds directly in the ground where they are to grow, 1 inch deep. Corn thrives on heat and must be planted in full sun. Soil should be light or medium, and well drained. The row method and the hill method both have their champions. If you use the row method, leave 3 feet between rows and thin young plants to 9 to 12 inches apart when they show above the ground. If you prefer the hill method, space the hills 3 feet apart each way. Sow 6 or 7 seeds in each hill, and then thin the strongest looking seedlings to 3 to a hill when they are about 5 inches tall.

If you start corn extra early before the rains are over, plant half way down the side of 6-inch-deep furrows. This provides good drainage in case of rain and permits the soil to warm up more quickly. As the corn grows, fill in the furrow.

You won't get much corn if you string it out in single rows. Corn depends upon the wind for pollination, so it is important to plant several short parallel rows rather than one long one (or plant groups of several hills). Run the rows north to south for maximum sun.

CULTURE

If soil is thoroughly moist before planting, no irrigation will be needed until plants are 7 or 8 inches tall. At that time dig a 2-inch-deep trench around the hill (or alongside a row) and scatter in a balanced commercial fertilizer. Allow the hose to run slowly into the trenches to water in the fertilizer. No other feeding will be necessary, but continue to give plants plenty of water during the growing period. Be sure to deep-soak at tasseling, and again at the time silk appears.

When you see suckers appearing at the base of the corn stalks, just leave them alone; they are absolutely harmless, and, as a matter of fact, their removal might cause a setback to the plant.

You often hear talk of interplanting corn with various other vegetables. Modern hybrids are planted close together on narrow row spacings; this creates such deep shade that only fast maturing crops such as lettuce and radishes do well when interplanted.

It is a well-known fact that the best corn is that which has been picked just minutes before and cooked immediately. If you've never eaten fresh-picked corn-on-the-cob, you have missed one of the most outstanding taste treats known to man. Produce market corn simply is not in the same class. However, it is extremely important to remember that even fresh-picked corn is nothing to brag about if you don't harvest it at the proper time. After ears form, the kernels go from the watery stage (immature) to the milky stage (just right) to the tough stage (too starchy to be good) in the space of a single hot day, although in cool weather the milky stage may last for a week or so.

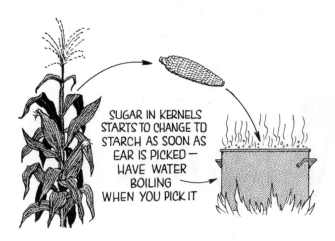

SUGAR IN KERNELS STARTS TO CHANGE TO STARCH AS SOON AS EAR IS PICKED— HAVE WATER BOILING WHEN YOU PICK IT

Test corn by peeling back some of the husk and puncturing it with your thumbnail. If milky juice squirts out, the ear should be picked immediately. Don't try to pull the ears off; instead, *twist*.

INSECT PESTS

Corn earworm is corn's most frequent enemy; it burrows through the silk and feeds on kernels near the tip of the ear. An excellent method of control is to spray silks with sevin when they appear, and again one week later.

cucumbers

You can grow cucumbers as big as blackjacks or as small as your little finger ... shaped like baby blimps or fat cigars or even like lemons ... smooth ones and "warty" ones ... for slicing or for pickling. All cucumbers — regardless of type — are rapid growers (55 to 70 days) and they don't need pampering. They do require some elbow room, but not so much as you might think.

CHARACTERISTICS

Cucumbers are members of the vine-like cucurbit family, a group of plants that includes melons, pumpkins, and squashes.

Cucumbers are easiest to grow in large gardens with plenty of open, sunny space. However, if your garden is short on "sprawling room," economy of space can be achieved by training the vines upward on trellises. Or, for an unusual patio plant, grow lemon cucumbers in a tub.

Regional considerations: Can be grown successfully in most sections of the U.S. so long as certain heat requirements are met. They do not like dry air and winds, and extremely moist air may cause mildew.

Recommended varieties: The newly introduced hybrids are so productive and disease resistant that there is little reason to plant the old standard varieties. *Slicers* (can also be pickled while small): Burpee Hybrid, Table Treat, Surecrop, Triumph. *Picklers:* Crispy, Spartan Dawn. Two oddities, very popular in the West, are Lemon (named for its yellow color and lemon shape), and Armenian Yard Long, an oriental or "Serpent" cucumber.

PLANTING INSTRUCTIONS

When to plant: In most regions, it is the accepted practice to sow seeds 1 or 2 weeks after average date of last frost. A better way to determine when you should plant cucumbers is to choose your seed, planting time, and planting method with the idea in mind of bringing the plant to maturity so that it will ripen during the warmest months of the year.

How to plant: Cucumbers do their best in a rich, sandy loam. They are usually grown in hills spaced 4 to 6 feet apart each way. When planting, bury a shovelful of manure and 2 handfuls of commercial fertilizer 12 to 16 inches deep in the planting hill. Place 5 or 6 seeds 1 inch deep in each hill, the pointed ends of the seeds down. As the plants grow, select the best, most evenly spaced 2 or 3 plants in each hill, removing the rest. Another method is to sow the seed 2 inches apart in rows above furrows which are spaced 4 feet apart. Water can be run into the furrows to give a cool, moist root-run for the plants, and to help maintain a cool atmosphere during hot weather.

In the Pacific Northwest, in fog belt areas, in Rocky Mountain states, and in other localities with a limited growing season, it is a good practice to start cucumber seeds early indoors in bands or compressed peat pots. To plant outdoors earlier than usual, sow 2 seeds at one time, one deeper than the other. If the seedling from the shallowly sown seed is frosted, there will be a second, later plant to take its place. If the first seedling survives, an earlier crop will result. Early plantings can also be protected with various coverings.

Home gardeners have invented all sorts of ingenious methods of overcoming soil and irrigation difficulties with cucumbers and squash; one is that of planting the seed around a container (a large can or square box can be used) punched or drilled with holes in the bottom and sunk in the middle of the hill. Water is slowly and evenly distributed to the plant roots. This method is especially valuable in hot, dry regions and on slopes.

A barrel, a wooden tub, or even a box will serve as a growing ground for cucumbers. The soil mixture should be rich — equal parts of sandy loam and rotted manure are ideal. These methods can be used to grow early crops in the greenhouse or any other heated indoor place suitable for plants.

CULTURE

Cucumber vines are fairly light in weight, and they respond well to training on wires, trellises, stakes, or even chicken wire. Letting them climb will not only save space, but will also result in a cleaner, better crop. Allow the center stem to grow as high as your climbing device will permit, and then pinch it off. Train the laterals sideways; some may have to be pinched back, but as much of their growth as possible should be retained, since the best fruit is borne on the lateral stems. Exercise care when making a tie, as the stems are somewhat brittle.

A feeding with liquid fertilizer between the young plant and fruit-setting stage will help to give you an outstanding crop. After feeding or watering, cultivate (lightly) as long as the size of the plant permits, to produce a fine surface mulch and to keep down weeds.

You may harvest cucumbers from time to time, whenever you wish, regardless of their size. It is important, however, to pick them before they mature, while they are still dark green.

INSECT PESTS

Cucumber beetle is the cucumber's most frequent enemy. The Eastern variety of this tiny beetle can be identified by the 3 black stripes down its wing covers; the Western type (diabrotica) has 12 black spots on the wings. They not only feed on the plant, but also can spread bacterial wilt, a fatal cucumber disease for which there is no known cure. The larva of the beetle also does damage, boring into the roots. Fortunately, cucumber beetle is easily controlled by dusting with diazinon or sevin. (Dusts are preferable to sprays, since moisture can cause mildew on cucumber plants.) Cucumber beetle will usually show up while plants are young.

Pickleworm is another bothersome adversary of the cucumber, particularly in the Southeastern states. It is ½ to ¾ inch long, and feeds on just about any part of the vine. Go after them early; any fruits that have already been entered by these worms had best be picked and disposed of. Weekly dustings with malathion, sevin, or diazinon will give effective control, and will serve a double purpose by killing any aphids that might be present.

Red spider mite can be controlled with guthion or diazinon.

Caution: Be sure to follow precautions on labels when using any of the above-mentioned chemicals.

eggplant

If you are seeking variety for your garden, the eggplant should receive your consideration — provided, of course, that the taste of this unusual vegetable appeals to you. Its culture is somewhat like that of the tomato, and, although it is no match for its round red relative in popularity, eggplant is the hands-down winner when it comes to beauty.

CHARACTERISTICS

This heat-loving relative to the tomato and the pepper makes a handsome addition to any garden. The plant grows to about 2 feet. Its large, shiny, purplish black fruit makes a unique and exciting end product (try it in a tub as a patio ornamental). Four plants will give you a crop of about 12 eggplants — enough to supply your family for several months if you store your surplus in a cool place. Eggplants bruise easily, so handle them carefully.

Eggplant will grow well in the same soil and exposure given to peppers and tomatoes, though it is a heavier feeder and more exacting than either of these crops, requiring longer to mature and being more easily affected by cold weather.

Regional considerations: Grows best in areas where it will have a long, warm growing season. Does not do well in many sections of the Pacific Northwest.

Recommended varieties: Black Beauty, Black Magic, Burpee Hybrid, Italian (Early Long Purple).

PLANTING INSTRUCTIONS

When to plant: Set young plants outdoors as soon as all danger of frost has passed.

How to plant: The eggplant is often a shy and uneven germinator, the seed sometimes taking as long as 3 to 4 weeks to germinate. Also it takes about 10 weeks from time of sowing seed in winter until plant-out time. For these reasons, and also because it takes but a few plants to provide an abundant supply of eggplants, home gardeners will generally be better off if they purchase a few young plants from a nursery.

If you prefer to start your own seed, your best bet is to sow them ⅛ inch deep in compressed peat pots, and then plant them — pots and all — at the proper time. In this way, there will be no danger of dirt falling away from roots when transplanting, which can be ruinous to this vegetable. Space young plants 36 inches apart in a warm, sunny place in the garden. If you are planting enough for several rows, leave 36 inches between rows. Soil should be loose, fertile, and well-drained.

CULTURE

From seeding to fruiting, the important thing is to keep eggplants growing steadily, since checks in growth result in inferior quality of fruit and a reduced crop. After the plants are established, feed once every 6 weeks with a balanced commercial fertilizer. Water every 10 days and cultivate afterward, thereby keeping the soil uniformly moist.

In order to prevent eggplant from setting too many fruits, the terminal growths on the stems, as well as some of the blossoms, should be pinched off. Three to six fruits are sufficient for a plant.

The fruits can be harvested from the time they are ⅓ grown until they are fully ripe. Never wait until the eggplant starts to lose its glossy shine, as it will be too tough for good eating. Seeds become bitter in overripe fruit.

INSECT PESTS

Colorado potato beetle can defoliate young plants. Control with rotenone, sevin, or diazinon. Eggplant lacebug, a troublesome pest in the South, feeds on the underside of leaves. Dust or spray with malathion. If aphids infest foliage, control them with rotenone or malathion *(note label precautions).*

Wilt diseases of the same types that attack tomatoes and potatoes will sometimes affect eggplant. The only "cure" is to try to avoid it by rotating crops and not growing eggplant where tomatoes or potatoes have been grown in the past three years.

 **herbs**

The smallest vegetable patch can afford to give room to herbs. A patch of ground 2 by 4 feet is large enough to grow most of the herbs the average family can use. If even this small space is impossible, plant a pot or two on the door step, in a tub on the patio, or in a window box. The result will please and delight you, and you'll have fun working new flavor twists into your meals.

For gardeners and cooks especially, herbs have a timeless appeal. Their fragrance, flavor, and healing qualities are woven into the rich tapestry of Biblical stories, ancient classics, quaint herbals, and scientific works. The ancestors of some of our most useful landscape plants, such as rosemary, date back at least as far as the beginning of recorded history. And when modern cooks use basil, oregano, thyme, or one of the other culinary herbs, they're bearing out Charlemagne's conviction that "an herb is the praise of cooks."

Yet with all this background of antiquity, herbs are remarkably up-to-date. They are and always have been food connoisseurs' favorites. On these pages, rather than to discuss all of the many different types of herbs that are used for everything from sachets to medicinal purposes, we will concentrate on some of the basic cooking herbs. (Also, see the cooking chart on page 70.)

HOW TO GROW

An herb garden belongs in full sun. A lean, barren soil will do very nicely for most kinds — too rich a soil makes plants run to foliage and dissipates their flavor. If your soil tends toward acidity, add lime.

Most of the annual herbs can be sown after the weather warms up, in the ground where they are to grow. Sow, thin, cultivate in the same manner as you do other vegetables.

Perennial herbs are usually sown in seed boxes and transplanted to flats or pots, from which they are planted into the garden. Many of them, such as rosemary and marjoram, are propagated from cuttings as well as seed. Tarragon can be grown from cuttings only.

HOW TO HARVEST

Herbs should be harvested when the flavor-bearing oils are richest and most concentrated. With herbs being grown for their leaves, this point is reached just as the flower buds begin to open or after the first flower has unfolded. If possible, choose a summer day which promises to be hot, and cut the herbs in the early morning while the dew is still on them.

The cut branches should be taken indoors and washed, then shaken dry. Next, strip the leaves from the stem, remove the flower heads, and place the leaves loosely and thinly on trays with wire mesh bottoms, through which air can freely circulate. The room in which the leaves are dried or "cured" should be warm and dry, with no direct sunlight reaching the trays. Stir the leaves each morning for 4 or 5 days, or until they are completely dry, then put them in air-tight containers, such as glass jars. Hanging herbs from rafters is unsanitary, since they collect dust, and drying outdoors blackens and shrivels the leaves.

BASIL

Sweet basil is a bushy East Indian annual that is easy to grow. The light yellow-green leaves and tender tips are spicy and flower-like in flavor and odor. A few plants can be potted in the fall and brought indoors for winter use. Use fresh or dried.

Culture: Sun, average moisture, light and well drained soil. Plant seeds each month for a steady supply of basil. Pinch out tips to keep plant bushy. Keep flowers cut. Plants will produce two crops a year.

BAY

This is actually a mild-climate tree (sweet bay or laurel), the leaves of which are used as herbs.

Culture: This tree is frequently grown in large tubs in the patio, or near an entryway. Many gardeners keep the head clipped in a rounded form.

DILL

Dill is an annual whose leaves and heads are used fresh or dried in making pickles; the dried leaves and flower heads are valued by some Europeans, particularly the people of Sweden, for flavoring boiled lamb or mutton.

Culture: Broadcast seed in a sunny position in spring after danger of frosts. Thin the plants to 12 or 15 inches apart when they are 2 to 3 inches high. Dill transplants badly and should not be sown in flats.

MARJORAM

Sweet marjoram was one of the most popular herbs of Colonial days. It is a bushy little plant about 2 feet high with soft foliage and white flowers in knotted clusters. Use leaves fresh or dried. Treat this herb as an annual in cold winter areas.

Culture: Likes full sun, fairly moist soil. Keep blossoms cut off and plant trimmed to prevent woody growth. Propagate from seed, cuttings, or root divisions.

MINT

There are many kinds of mint in popular use. The most common is the perennial *spearmint*, which grows to 2 feet tall and has dark green leaves with leafy spikes of purplish flowers. Use it fresh.

Culture: Full sun or partial shade. With adequate moisture it spreads rapidly by underground stems. It is advisable to contain the roots in a box or pot, to keep them from taking over the garden. Propagate from runners.

OREGANO

Also known as *pot marjoram*, this hardy perennial grows to 2½ feet tall. Medium-sized leaves are oval shaped; blooms are purplish pink. Although oregano is best fresh, you can also use it dried.

Culture: Sun, medium rich soil, good drainage, average watering. Keep trimmed to prevent flowering. Replant every 3 years.

PARSLEY

Parsley is the one herb no garden, though it be only an apartment window box, should fail to include. The 6 to 10-inch-high plants make as handsome a green edging or border plant for the herb or vegetable garden as anyone could wish. Use parsley either fresh or dried. Parsley is a biennial which lives over winter except where weather is severe. Old plants go to seed in late spring, so start anew from seeds each year.

Culture: Sun, good soil, average watering. Buy plants at a nursery, or plant in place from seed. Soak seed in warm water 24 hours before planting. Sow 10 to 12 inches apart.

ROSEMARY

Rosemary has a sweet fragrant scent suggestive of nutmeg and pine needles. The savor is warm and pungent, and the shrubs themselves are ornamental. Foliage is gray-green, flowers pale blue. Shrubs reach 3 to 5 feet tall, but the spreading form (prostrate rosemary) is only 15 inches high.

Culture: Full sun, well drained gravelly soil slightly on the lean side. Drought resistant. Layers easily, or can be propagated from cuttings.

SAGE

This is a shrubby gray-leafed perennial with blue flowers. Plants grow 2 feet high and furnish 2 crops per season.

Culture: Sun, poor soil. Fairly drought resistant. Cut it back after bloom. Fertilize if you cut it continually. Divide every 3 to 4 years. Propagate from cuttings or layers, or grow from seed (germinates easily).

SAVORY

There are two kinds — a summer and a winter type. Most popular is the summer savory, an 18-inch annual which grows easily from seed. Leaves are narrow and green; flowers pinkish white. Entire plant is extremely fragrant. Use fresh or dried.

Culture: Savory likes full sun, an adequate amount of moisture, and poor soil. Keep it clipped. Lift and divide in early summer or late fall. Clip at the start of the flowering season for drying.

TARRAGON

Tarragon plants are 2-foot perennials that are good for about 4 years. New plants are not readily available; get them from an herb specialist.

Culture: This hardy plant thrives in poor soil. Give it some sun and normal watering. New plants can be started easily from divisions in the spring.

THYME

There are many kinds of thyme, all perennials and easy to grow. Plants grow 8 to 12 inches high, with small green leaves and tiny lavender flowers.

Culture: Plant in sun in light, sandy soil that is moderately dry (thyme thrives in hot, dry places where most other plants fail). Prune after flowering. Replant every 3 years. Grows well from tip cuttings taken in spring. Grows easily from seed.

Kale

This loose-leafed member of the cabbage family is so exceedingly simple to grow that it should be a "must" for all home vegetable gardens. Cold weather doesn't faze it in the least; in fact, the flavor and crispness of the leaves are never better than when they have just been touched by a light frost. The plant is so attractive that it can enhance a flower border or even occupy a plant tub with distinction.

CHARACTERISTICS

Kale is a hardy, low growing plant that performs best under cool conditions although it also does fairly well in summer. It furnishes greens to home gardeners during late fall and early winter months at a time when other leafy vegetables are scarce.

In the South and in other areas where winters are not extreme, it is grown all winter. Like Swiss chard, it can be harvested over a long period, the leaves being removed when they are needed.

Leaves may be boiled, like spinach, or used raw in salads and sandwiches.

If you prefer row planting, you will find that a single 20-foot row will give your family an adequate supply. However, so fascinating is the ornamental quality of the leaves that many a home gardener prefers to work kale into the flower beds rather than to use up valuable space in the vegetable garden. Many varieties have leaves that are densely curled, beautifully fringed, and plume-like; some are dark green and others have a bluish or even purplish cast. Try them in flower arrangements.

Regional considerations: Can be grown easily anywhere in the U. S.

Recommended varieties: Dwarf Blue Curled, Siberian.

PLANTING INSTRUCTIONS

When to plant: For a fall and early winter crop, sow seed in midsummer. Seeds grow to maturity in 60 to 80 days. Plantings in late winter or fall are also possible in mild-winter regions.

How to plant: Sow seeds ½ inch deep in soil that is well drained and rich in organic matter. If planting more than one row, leave 16 inches between rows. Thin plants to 20 inches apart (use thinned seedlings for greens).

CULTURE

Treat the growing plants in the same way as cabbage and other cole crops. Follow a regular watering program, and keep plants coming along with an occasional application of liquid fertilizer.

Kale can be harvested by: 1) cutting the outer leaves as they mature; or, 2) cutting the entire plant at one time. If you intend to use it exclusively as a cooked vegetable, you'll get the most out of each plant by using the first, or "cut-and-come-again" method. If you want to use it mainly in the raw form, it's best to follow the second method and use only the inside leaves, which are much superior to the outer ones.

INSECT PESTS

Kale is subject to the same pests that attack cabbage (especially aphids); see the section on cabbage for recommended controls.

kohlrabi

This excellent, little-known vegetable, often called the turnip cabbage, resembles a turnip but has a milder flavor considered superior to turnip by some people. The swollen stem which forms above the ground is delicious when eaten juicy and young, and has a "different" flavor.

CHARACTERISTICS

One of the most interesting members of the cabbage family. Kohlrabi's growing needs are the same as for cabbage and related crops, but the leaves and the enlarged stem base which forms above the ground have more the appearance of a turnip. It is a short-season crop that must be harvested when the enlarged stem reaches the size of a large egg. Kohlrabi grows rapidly from seed to maturity (55 to 60 days). Eat kohlrabi cooked like turnips, or raw. It is excellent sliced, like cucumbers, in a salad.

Regional considerations: Can be grown as a cool-season crop anywhere in the U. S.

Recommended varieties: Early White Vienna is the most commonly grown kohlrabi for home gardens. Early Purple Vienna is another popular variety; skin is purple, but flesh of the bulbous stem is creamy white, as is that of all kohlrabi.

PLANTING INSTRUCTIONS

When to plant: Sow seed beginning 2 weeks after average date of last frost, and follow with several plantings 2 weeks apart to provide a succession of tender, succulent roots over a long period. In mild climates, plant again in late fall and early winter.

How to plant: Sow seeds ½ inch deep in rows, with 18 inches between rows, and thin to 4 inches apart when seedlings are up. Plant in a sunny place, in rich soil. It is imperative, if your soil is only moderately fertile, to add a generous amount of organic matter prior to planting (well rotted manure is ideal).

CULTURE

Only a rich soil and rapid growth before hot weather will produce kohlrabi of good quality. Slow or checked growth results in tough, stringy, almost woody, swollen parts that are bitter and useless. Regular watering and several feedings with commercial fertilizers are necessary to keep the crop growing rapidly.

INSECT PESTS

Kohlrabi is generally free from both pests and diseases. If aphids cause trouble, dust or spray with rotenone.

lettuce

Lettuce is so easy to grow and can be planted in so many locations in the garden that no gardener anywhere should be without a constant supply. It is one of the easiest of all vegetables to grow from seed. There are many different kinds to choose from, and dedicated lettuce fanciers are often delighted to discover that they've found a hobby — searching the seed racks each planting season for new varieties to brighten the family salad bowl and surprise dinner guests.

CHARACTERISTICS

The 3 types of lettuce most commonly grown in home gardens in this country are head lettuce (crisphead and butterhead), leaf lettuce, and romaine (Cos) lettuce. All of them are cool-season crops, but it is possible to grow romaine — and, to a lesser extent, leaf lettuce — in summer, in all but the hottest climates. Plant rows of different varieties of all 3 kinds at intervals through the year to keep a continuous, varied supply coming on.

Lettuce is readily adaptable to many garden situations. If you have a flat or two of small plants on hand, you will find it easy to tuck them into odd corners, along paths, in the flower bed, in window boxes, in tubs near the back door, in between rows of maturing crops, in the spaces left when other vegetables are pulled out, or interplanted in rows of slower-growing crops.

Leaf lettuce is an exceptionally fast grower, reaching maturity from seed in about 45 days. Head lettuce and romaine types take 60 to 85 days.

Regional considerations: Lettuce is easy to grow anywhere in the U. S.

Recommended varieties: Choosing a list of the best lettuce varieties is an utter impossibility. There are hundreds of them, and if you grow them properly you just can't go wrong on any of them. Here are a few of the ones most commonly grown in home gardens: *Crisp head:* Great Lakes strains, Iceberg, Imperial strains. *Butterhead:* Buttercrunch (Bibb type), Dark Green Boston, Fordhook. *Loose leaf:* Black Seeded Simpson, Ruby (an attractive red), Salad Bowl, Prizehead, Grand Rapids. *Romaine:* Paris White Cos. Check your nurseryman for advice; some of the lesser-known types may do especially well in your area.

PLANTING INSTRUCTIONS

When to plant: For spring and early summer crops of the head and romaine types, make 3 small sowings indoors at weekly intervals, starting 2 weeks before average date of last frost. Set the young plants in the garden, all at one time if you wish, when frosts are over and ground has become workable. For still more successive crops, sow some seed out-of-doors at the same time young plants are set out. Successive crops are particularly necessary for head lettuce, which should not be left in the garden after it reaches maturity. Make two or three supplementary plantings in late summer; if you live in a mild-winter area, still further plantings can be made in fall and early winter.

Leaf lettuce grows so quickly from seed that the usual procedure is to sow seeds directly in the ground at 10-day intervals, starting after frost when ground becomes workable. Or, sow all your seeds in a single planting and harvest the outside leaves as the plants grow; this will give you leaf lettuce for many weeks.

How to plant: If you only wish to plant a small amount of lettuce, it is a good idea to purchase a few plants from a nursery and spot them in where you need them. But if quantity and variety are your goals, it's best to grow lettuce from seed. Either way, you will find that lettuce transplants easily and with little or no setback or shock.

Plant seeds ½ inch deep in rows, leaving 18 inches between the rows. Head lettuce and romaine should be set out or thinned to 12 inches apart. The same applies to leaf lettuce if you intend to pick the outer leaves over a long period; however, if you intend to harvest a whole plant at a time, plants need only be separated 4 inches. Space butterhead lettuce 3 to 5 inches apart.

Plant lettuce in any good, well-drained, loose soil (it need not be more than moderately rich). Choose a sunny location; however, if you live in an area where summers are hot and you are planning a summer crop, give them at least partial protection from midday sun with lath or some other shade device.

CULTURE

Generous and regular watering is essential during the growing period, especially in warm weather.

Because lettuce has a meager root system, heavy fertilizing after planting is not necessary. However, light applications of commercial fertilizer as a side dressing throughout the life of the plant will give good results, beginning right after plants are set out.

In some regions, birds will attack young lettuce before it has hardly emerged from the ground. If this is true where you live, you'll increase your chances if you forsake seed sowing out-of-doors and stick to starting seeds indoors, setting them out when they have begun to take on the look of sturdy young plants. Or, cover the seed rows with wire or light cloth.

Endive is actually a member of the chicory family, but we list it here because it is an excellent lettuce substitute and because its culture is so much like that of lettuce. It will stand more heat and grow faster in cold, rainy weather than lettuce, and it can therefore be grown in a wider range of climates. Endive (known as escarolle or chicory in certain sections) is usually planted in late summer. Later crops can be seeded in mild winter areas. Blanching improves flavor; bunch the leaves around the plant and tie with string. Green Curled is an excellent early variety (65 days from seed).

INSECT PESTS

Leafhoppers are a common enemy to lettuce everywhere in the U. S., not because of any chewing or boring damage but because they are carriers of plant diseases. Control with repeated applications of malathion or sevin when plants are young *(note label precautions)*.

Earwigs, the pincer-tailed night foragers, often feed on lettuce. If you have this pest, go after him with baits.

Use rotenone to control aphids on lettuce.

Set out baits to control snails and slugs, starting when plants are young.

melons

Muskmelon (cantaloupe) is by far the most popular melon for home gardens. A home grown muskmelon, of a home garden variety, is superior in every way — taste, texture, and aroma — to the best commercial offering. Whether your preference is muskmelon, watermelon, or one of the late types such as Honey Dew, be sure you can meet the three absolute essentials for successful melon growing: suitable climate, plenty of space, and a diligent watering program.

CHARACTERISTICS

There are two reasons why a home-grown muskmelon can walk off with all the honors when it is stacked against a commercial variety: 1) Several varieties have unusually tender, melt-in-your-mouth flesh. These varieties are passed up by commercial growers because they don't ship well. 2) The home-grown variety is generally sweeter because you pick it full-ripe. Unlike some other fruits, muskmelons do not increase in sweetness when picked green. In fact, their sugar content begins to drop soon after picking. Melons are members of the cucurbit family, vine crops which include — among others — squash and cucumbers. They are a very tender, warm-weather crop, and will not stand even a cold "snap," much less weather that is continually cold or cool.

It takes 75 to 95 days for muskmelon and watermelon to reach maturity from seed; late melons take 110 to 120 days.

Regional considerations: Muskmelons and watermelons are grown in most sections of the U. S., although watermelons are a particular favorite in the Southern states. The casabas and other late types are best grown in the South and in California.

The ideal melon climate has a long growing season, early season warmth, and warm nights as well as days. If melons are being grown commercially around you, you know you have the right climate for top production.

Recommended varieties: *Muskmelons:* Hearts of Gold, Supermarket Hybrid, Burpee Hybrid, Edisto, Delicious 51 (two of the best early types), Hales Best. *Late melons:* Honey Dew, Casaba Golden Beauty, Crenshaw, Persian. *Watermelons:* Sugar Baby (small, so-called "icebox varieties"), Crimson Sweet, Burpee's Fordhook F_1 Hybrid (moderate-sized, nearly round, up to 14 lbs.), Charleston Gray or Congo (Southeast), Klondike (West).

PLANTING INSTRUCTIONS

When to plant: Sow seeds 2 weeks after average date of last frost, with a careful eye on the seed-to-maturity date so you can be reasonably certain that hot weather will arrive by fruit-forming time.

Where less than 4 months are frost-free and summers are cool, start seeds indoors in peat pots or plant bands 4 to 6 weeks prior to average frost-free date.

How to plant: Melons do their best in a soil that is on the light and sandy side. Plant them in an open, sunny location. Lay out gently rounded, raised beds, 6 feet from center to center (allow 8 feet for watermelons). It is a good idea to bury 2

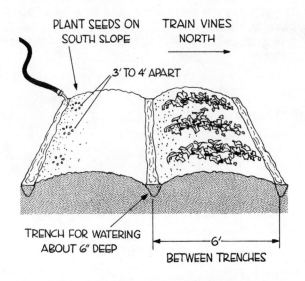

PLANT SEEDS ON SOUTH SLOPE   TRAIN VINES NORTH

3' TO 4' APART

TRENCH FOR WATERING ABOUT 6" DEEP

6' BETWEEN TRENCHES

inches of well-rotted manure 10 inches deep in the planting hills. On the south side of the bed, make a furrow (with a hoe) about 10 inches wide and 6 inches deep. (South side catches maximum sun and is warmer.) Run water into the furrows until they are filled. Every 3 feet along the furrow (again, allow

8 feet for watermelons) scrape away about 1 inch of soil in an 8 to 10-inch circle about 6 inches away from the furrow. (This soil has been thoroughly moistened by the first irrigation.) Scatter 6 or 7 seeds in the circle, place ½ inch of the moist soil over them, and press down with the back of your hoe or your hands. Add the remaining ½ inch of soil, but do not firm it down. It's good insurance against too rapid drying out of the seed bed to add a light mulch.

Unless the weather is abnormally hot, no additional water will be needed until the seed has germinated. If irrigation is necessary, keep the water in the furrow; avoid flooding the seeded areas.

As soon as the plants are established, and before they begin to crowd, thin out, leaving 2 plants to the hill. If the roots of the 2 plants which are to remain will be disturbed by the removal of the unwanted ones, cut off the latter with a knife.

CULTURE

As the plants grow, train them away from the irrigation furrow and gradually work the furrow away from the plants — a distance of 12 inches or more. In this way both vines and fruit are on high ground and are never wet.

Do not keep the soil soaked. A continuous supply of moisture in the root zone, 8 to 12 inches deep, is best maintained by frequent but not excessive irrigations.

Scatter a balanced commercial fertilizer in the irrigation furrow every 6 weeks.

Perhaps the only really puzzling thing about melons is knowing exactly when to pick them. Here are some clues to indicate ripeness: *Muskmelon:* At "full slip", when stem comes off cleanly, leaving a concave depression. *Persian, Crenshaw:* Try the aroma test. Sniff the blossom end; if it smells sweet and ripe, the melon is ready. Crenshaw can be dead ripe yet have a green skin. *Honeydew, Casaba:* When rind has turned completely yellow. *Watermelon:* There is no fool-proof method. Your best bet is to try the thump test (a firm rapping with a knuckle). If you get a "ping" wait a day or so and try again; a muffled "plunk" means the watermelon is probably ready.

INSECT PESTS

Same as for cucumber.

mustard greens

Mustard shouldn't be confused with the prepared mustard that peps up hot dogs. Mustard greens are one of the most versatile vegetables. Yet, for some reason, this excellent leaf crop never has been a home garden favorite except in some regions of the South. It is a fast and easy grower, and if you try it, you will probably be happily surprised.

CHARACTERISTICS

Mustard is an annual, the young leaves of which make a delicious and sharp addition to green salads, or they can be cooked as greens. It grows from seed in 35 to 40 days, which puts it right up with radish as one of the top speed-burners in the entire vegetable league.

Regional considerations: Mustard can be grown anywhere in the U.S.

Recommended varieties: Southern Giant Curled, Tendergreen, Green Wave, Florida Broadleaf.

PLANTING INSTRUCTIONS

When to plant: Sow seed in early spring, as soon as the ground can be worked. Mustard withstands light frost. Plant again in late summer for fall use.

In mild-winter areas, plant again in fall and winter. Mustard matures so rapidly that several sowings a season are required for a succession of young greens.

How to plant: Sow the seeds ½ inch deep in short rows or small patches, just as you would radishes. Thin plants to stand 6 inches apart.

CULTURE

Keep plants growing fast with ample amounts of water. Fertilizer isn't necessary if your soil is reasonably rich.

Harvest leaves continuously as they approach maturity. By keeping the plants well-watered and cut back, flowering and seed production is delayed.

INSECT PESTS

Same as for turnips.

okra

If your garden will grow good sweet corn, it will grow good okra. It grows best where summers are hot and humid, and is quite popular in the South. The plant is a space-taker, so if your garden is small you'll be better off trying something else.

CHARACTERISTICS

Okra is a tender crop, quite easy to grow during the summer months and yet 'seldom found in home gardens except in the South. Plants grow 5 feet tall (dwarf varieties 3 feet) and rows must be spaced 3 feet apart.

Regional considerations: Can be grown anywhere in the U.S.

Recommended varieties: Louisiana Green Velvet, Perkin's Mammoth, Emerald, Red River, Clemson Spineless, Dwarf Green Long Pod.

PLANTING INSTRUCTIONS

When to plant: Sow seed when frosts are over and ground has begun to warm up.

How to plant: Soak seed for 24 hours before planting, to speed up germination. Plant seeds ½ inch deep in rows 36 inches apart, in the warmest spot in the garden. When seedlings are up, thin

them to 15 inches apart. For best results, add some manure to soil before planting.

CULTURE

Water regularly, and apply a commercial fertilizer at least once during the growing season.

The edible pods are ready for harvest about 60 days from date of sowing seed (harvest 4 to 6 days after the flower opens). Pick the ripened pods every 2 or 3 days; pods left on the plant to over-ripen will be tough and stringy, and the picking season will be shortened as the plant's strength is sapped.

INSECT PESTS

Corn earworm is okra's chief pest, eating holes in the pods. Apply sevin dust or spray before pods form.

If aphids or Japanese beetle cause trouble, dust or spray with malathion. (*Caution:* Do not use malathion after pods start to form.)

onions & family

Onions are a large and happy family, so easy to grow that every home gardener should try them. Most well-known kinds are green onions, dry onions, garlic, leeks, chives, and shallots. There are some slight differences in culture, but they all share the same uncomplicated set of growing rules: Never let them dry out, fertilize them occasionally, and be patient.

CHARACTERISTICS

Onions are hardy vegetables that do their best if they have fairly consistent weather conditions throughout their growing period, with no temperature extremes. The kinds that most home gardeners grow are:

Green onions: They grow quickly and easily from sets (small bulbs) and are an ideal catch crop to tuck in wherever a little space is available. Green onions also grow quickly and economically from seeds of Evergreen Bunching; each seed sends up 2 or 3 shoots upon sprouting.

Dry onions: Dry onions are an important staple crop. They are grown from seed or from sets. You have a choice of many varieties (see below).

Garlic: One or two garlic bulbs (the small sections or "cloves" separated) will supply the average family with enough garlic to flavor favorite salads and other dishes throughout the year.

Shallots: This clove-producing type is similar to garlic. Young leaves as well as cloves are used as seasoning.

Leeks: These are frequently grown as a substitute for green onions in fall and winter. Both leaves and roots are edible.

Chives: The green tops, when chopped up, are highly prized by gourmets as a seasoning. Cut tops when you need them, and chives keep on growing.

Regional considerations: Grown throughout the U.S.

Recommended varieties: *Green onions:* White sets are considered by many to produce the best green onions. *Dry onions:* Spring planting: Early Yellow Globe, Sweet Spanish, Red Wethersfield. Fall or winter planting: Bermuda, Granex, Crystal White Wax. *Leeks:* Giant Musselburgh, and Broad London.

PLANTING INSTRUCTIONS

When to plant: Plant onion sets all winter and up through April in mild climates; plant them in earliest spring in harsh-winter climates. Or, sow seed in early spring.

How to plant: Onions like a rich, loose, well-drained soil, and a sunny location. Plant the various types as follows:

Green onions: Plant the sets 1 to 1½ inches deep and 1 to 2 inches apart.

Dry onions: Sow the seed ½ inch deep and ¼ inch apart in rows 15 to 18 inches apart. Most varieties will reach maturity in 95 to 110 days. When the onions are about the size of a pencil, they can be transplanted to 3 or 4 inches apart. When doing this, the tops should be cut off half way down, and the roots slightly trimmed.

Garlic: Cloves should be planted 1 to 1½ inches deep and 2 to 3 inches apart in rows 12 inches apart. You'll have good-sized bulbs in 90 days.

Shallots: Planting instructions same as for garlic.

Leeks: Start seed of leeks in flats of loam, and transplant to permanent positions when plants are 2 inches high. They should be set 3 to 4 inches apart in rows 15 to 18 inches apart. (Seed can be sown directly in the ground, but results are not quite as good.) Once the plants take hold, cultivate often, drawing the soil toward the plants, and water regularly. Leeks are blanched by putting over each plant a collar of waterproof paper 3 inches high and about 2 inches in diameter. As the plant grows, the collar is moved up. Leeks require about 100 days from seed to maturity, and they should be dug before hard frosts appear.

Chives: Buy pots of young chive seedlings and separate them by pulling apart gently. Try growing some in window boxes, or plant several in a small pot and grow them indoors by a sunny window.

CULTURE

Moderate temperatures and adequate moisture are required to produce a good crop. The most important rule of onion culture is never to allow the soil in which onions are growing to dry out completely. The steady growth of onions should not be checked in any way.

Green onions are pulled as needed and are rarely allowed to go to seed. Dry onions are harvested after the tops have ripened. It is important not to pull them before the outer skin has dried, since immature onions bruise easily and do not keep well.

The common practice is to break or crush the stems if there are signs of flower heads. When the stems are dry, dig the bulbs, which can be left on top of the ground to cure and dry for several days.

INSECT PESTS

Onion thrips are pests throughout the country. Adults and larvae suck out juices from the plants. Control with malathion (*note label precautions*).

Onion maggot, most commonly found in the Northern part of the country, burrows into the onion bulbs. Best control is achieved by treating the soil prior to planting time with diazinon wettable powder.

parsnips

If you are one of the relatively few people who find parsnips to their liking, there's no reason why you can't grow your own. Just remember two things: It requires about 4 months to grow from seed, and during all this time it may be taking up a considerable amount of valuable garden space.

CHARACTERISTICS

Parsnips are a root crop, and their culture is much the same as for carrots and beets. It is necessary to prepare the soil deeply prior to planting, as some varieties are 15 inches long.

Regional considerations: Parsnips can be grown anywhere in the U.S.

Recommended varieties: Improved Hollow Crown, All American, Harris Model.

PLANTING INSTRUCTIONS

When to plant: In cold winter areas, plant seeds in late spring, let them grow through summer, harvest them in fall, and leave the excess in the ground to be dug as needed all winter. In mild-climate areas, sow seed in fall and harvest in spring. (In mild regions you should never leave parsnips in the ground past maturity even in winter, as they will become tough and woody).

How to plant: Sow seeds ½ inch deep in rows 3 feet apart, and thin to 5 inches apart in the row. Parsnips must have a loose soil that has been worked to a depth of 18 inches.

CULTURE

Follow the same growing techniques as for carrots and beets.

INSECT PESTS

Parsnips are remarkably free from insects and diseases.

peas

Tender, green, deliciously fresh peas are to the spring vegetable garden what daffodils are to the flower garden. It is "their" season when days become warmer and longer, yet the soil and atmosphere retain their cooling moisture, so important to peas. They are easy to grow when conditions are right, and they grow from seed to harvest stage in a real hurry. If you are short on garden space, try the bush varieties — easy to care for and surprisingly productive.

CHARACTERISTICS

Peas and beans have an obvious botanical relationship, but little else in common. Whereas beans are a tender crop that demand warm weather, peas are hardy and require a cool growing season.

If you have the space, and don't mind the extra care, you can grow the tall-growing types and train them up trellises, wires, strings, chicken wire, or stakes. These 4 and 5-foot climbers produce abundantly and can be picked over a longer period of time than the bush types. The latter, however, are very popular in small gardens, since they do not take up as much space and do not require staking.

You sometimes hear talk of "smooth-seeded and wrinkled-seeded peas — which are best?" The answer is that wrinkled-seeded peas are best. As a matter of fact, it is hard to find a smooth-seeded variety on the seed racks.

For an unusual taste treat, try growing a few sugar peas (Chinese Snow Peas). Pick them young and cook the pods like snap beans, without shelling.

Most varieties of peas will grow from seed to maturity in 60 to 80 days.

Regional considerations: Can be grown in most sections of the U.S.

Recommended varieties: *Tall:* Alderman, Miragreen, Wando (heat resistant), Freezonian. *Bush:* Little Marvel, Morse's No. 55, Morse's Progress No. 9, Burpee's Blue Bantam, Burpeeana Early. *Sugar peas:* Melting Sugar (tall), Dwarf Gray Sugar (bush). Check with your nurseryman for other outstanding varieties that grow well in your area.

PLANTING INSTRUCTIONS

When to plant: Peas are hardy enough to plant in early spring as soon as the ground can be worked, or in fall where winters are mild and spring days are too warm for their comfort.

How to plant: Sow seeds 2 inches deep in a deep, rich, medium loam which is light enough to drain well, yet is substantial enough to retain moisture if weather turns warm. Soil must be non-acid. Peas rot in cold, moist ground; good drainage and careful preparation of the soil are imperative. Seed should be planted more shallowly in winter or in heavy soil (½ inch), although you'll be better off, if your soil is heavy, to bring in some topsoil and build some raised beds for raising peas and other vegetables as well. Spergon seed protectant helps to prevent peas from rotting.

Moisten the ground thoroughly before planting, and do not water again until after the seedlings have broken through the surface. A light mulch will help conserve moisture underneath.

Leave 24 inches between rows, thinning young seedlings so that plants stand 2 inches apart.

Peas are short-lived, and successive plantings several days apart are needed to supply an average family. Many gardeners plant early, midseason, and late varieties all at the same time rather than bother with successive plantings.

CULTURE

Peas are not as heavily fertilized as some crops, but those grown in a light, sandy loam yield better returns when fed with a complete commercial fertilizer. Fertilizers with a high nitrogen content should be avoided, since they over-stimulate the plants, causing them to become lush, sappy, shy on producing, and liable to attacks from pests and diseases.

If the weather becomes warm and the atmosphere dry, peas will need water, which should be supplied in furrows between rows. Overhead watering encourages mildew. Cultivation should follow watering to preserve a surface mulch, but it must be shallow to avoid root injury.

Provide support for climbing peas as soon as tendrils begin to form. Pinch back the ends of the vines and thin out shoots on plants that are running heavily to vegetative growth. This may often be a necessity in too-rich soils or with over-stimulated plants.

Once peas start bearing, regularly pick *all* pods as they mature to keep the vines producing and to lengthen the picking season. Vines are easily injured; steady them with one hand while breaking off pods with the other.

Cook peas (or shell them and freeze them) as soon as possible after picking — preferably within 2 or 3 hours — for maximum sweetness and flavor.

INSECT PESTS

The most common and persistent pests of peas are the pea aphids, which suck sap from the plant and cause it to wilt. Pea weevil, especially prevalent in the West, is a tiny beetle that feeds in the blossoms and lays small white eggs on the young pods. The larvae then bore down through egg shell and pod and enter the developing peas.

There are a number of sprays and dusts that will control pea aphids, and you also can choose from several that will eliminate pea weevil. Try diazinon — it will do them both in.

 **peppers**

Peppers are grown in much the same way as eggplants and tomatoes. They introduce variety into the garden and the diet, and have a pictorial as well as practical value. Handsomely-foliaged, bushy plants covered with white flowers or with shining green or red peppers can be just as attractive as many a flowering plant grown for ornament alone.

CHARACTERISTICS

There are two kinds of peppers: 1) sweet, and 2) hot. The sweet ones (bell peppers) are green when young, usually turning red at maturity — but regardless of when picked, they are sweet. The hot ones (chili peppers) are smaller than the bell type. They are also green (sometimes yellowish) when young, turning red at maturity — but they are always hot.

It takes only 6 to 8 pepper plants (including only 1 or 2 of the hot kind) to satisfy the needs of the average family. For this reason, it is better to buy a few young plants than to grow them from seed. Ask your dealer for a mosaic-resistant variety. This is a serious disease which is difficult to prevent in standard varieties.

In addition to their attractive fruit, peppers have a neat upright shape that helps them to fit into many situations. They can be grown in flower beds, or tucked into odd, sunny corners. They are naturals for growing in tubs on the patio.

Regional considerations: Peppers can be grown in most sections in the U.S. Climate conditions under which they do their best are the same as for eggplants and tomatoes. Peppers are particularly receptive to humidity.

Recommended varieties: *Sweet*: Burpee's Fordhook, California Wonder, Yolo Wonder, Keystone Resistant Giant. *Hot:* Long Red Cayenne, Red Chili, Hungarian Yellow Wax, Mexican Chili (for making chili powder), Chili Jalapeno.

PLANTING INSTRUCTIONS

When to plant: Set out transplants after all danger of frost is past.

How to plant: Space young plants 18 inches apart, allowing 24 inches between rows. Ideal soil is a light, warm, rich loam that is well-drained and yet not too fast-drying. Choose a sunny location.

Peppers must be transplanted with care, as a precaution against growth check. If you prefer to grow your own peppers from seed, use compressed peat pots. Sow seeds ½ inch deep in the pots, 8 to 10 weeks ahead of planting time. Plant the "pot" and all — roots will grow right on through the compressed peat-and-fertilizer shell with no setback.

CULTURE

After the peppers are established, make wide furrows, 4 inches deep between the rows, or if growing in odd-shaped beds, make basins around each plant for irrigation. Thorough watering every 10 days, followed by cultivation and weeding, if necessary, is essential during the warm active growing season.

One or two feedings with commercial fertilizer between the time the plants are 6 to 8 inches tall and up until the blossoming period, will aid in producing the rapid growth demanded by peppers. It takes 65 to 85 days for most varieties to reach maturity from the time transplants are set out.

Plants grown in a sandy soil that is on the dry side will mature more rapidly than those grown in heavier, more retentive soils, but will not be of such high quality.

Pick the peppers when they ripen, thereby relieving the plant and releasing energy for further fruit production and a longer season. Bell peppers are ready to be picked when they are firm and crisp to the touch. Many people believe they have a better flavor if picked while still green. Hot peppers that you intend to dry should be allowed to ripen on the vine.

INSECT PESTS

Pepper weevil is a sometime pest in the Southern sections of the country. Dust or spray with sevin. Wash peppers thoroughly before eating, particularly around the stem end.

Set out bait for cutworms before planting and while plants are still young.

Although aphids and other pests may show up occasionally, peppers rate high on the list as a relatively pest-free vegetable. If mosaic shows up in a plant (leaves look cupped, yellow and hard, plant is stunted), pull the plant out before insect carriers spread the disease.

potatoes

Potatoes are the most popular dinner-plate vegetable of them all. Nevertheless, as you can see by the short shrift we've given them below, it is a sad fact that the average home gardener should stick to buying his "spuds" from the local markets. They are space-eaters and they can fall prey to many diseases.

CHARACTERISTICS

Potatoes are tubers that grow underground at the end of short stems. Their greatest need is a long growing season (about 4 months) with continuous cool weather.

Sweet potatoes are exceptionally tricky for the average home gardener to grow, and are not recommended as a home garden crop.

Regional considerations: Potatoes are grown in many sections of the U.S., but they prefer regions where they can be grown over long, cool seasons with temperatures that seldom rise above 65°.

Recommended varieties: Potatoes are grown from certified, disease-free seed potatoes. (Cut them into chunky pieces 1½ inches square, each with at least one eye.) Each section of the country has certain potato varieties that are best adapted to its climate. See your local nurseryman for advice as to which kinds are available in your area.

PLANTING INSTRUCTIONS

When to plant: Get potatoes in the ground as early in spring as the ground can be worked. If your area has a long, cool fall, you can plant them in June or July; cool weather will have arrived by the time tubers start to develop.

How to plant: First, saturate the soil. Then place the potato pieces cut side down, 4 inches deep (6 inches in very light soil), and 12 to 18 inches apart, depending on the size of the variety, in rows spaced 24 inches apart.

CULTURE

Potato roots (not the potatoes themselves) need constant moisture; ideally, however, you should not have to water the young plants during the weeks that they are putting down their roots and becoming established. Once they are up and growing, give them an occasional soaking.

Early, or "new" potatoes can be dug when the tops begin to flower. The main crop should be dug when the tops die down.

INSECT PESTS

Potatoes are subject to an eye-popping number of pests and diseases; fortunately, most of them are localized to certain areas. Consult your county agricultural agent for controls recommended for your area.

You can help to control potato tuber moth — which lays its eggs in cracks in the ground — by following a regular irrigation program so the soil won't dry out and crack.

radishes

The two great virtues of the radish are its ease of culture and rapidity of growth. Most varieties mature with a speed that is downright astonishing. Radishes are wonderfully useful as a "catch" crop between slow-growing vegetables, and it is a good idea to keep a few seeds handy at all times to sow them as needed in miscellaneous fashion.

CHARACTERISTICS

All root crops are easy to grow, but easiest of all is the radish. There are some varieties that are ready to be pulled in only 22 days. Most varieties take about a month, and long-rooted winter types require 55 days.

As mentioned above, radishes make a fine "catch" crop. They are also frequently used as a "nurse" crop with other root crops that are slower or more difficult to germinate, such as carrots and parsnips. Seeds of both crops are sown at the same time, the radishes coming up first and breaking the soil for the slower vegetables. Quick harvesting is necessary in this case, in order that the growth of the more important crop will not be checked because of lack of growing space. (For good eating quality, radishes should *always* be harvested promptly, as they become pithy when left in the ground too long.)

Regional considerations: Radishes will perform well anywhere. Even in regions where outside winter culture is impossible, radishes can easily be forced in greenhouses, coldframes, or sunny windows.

Recommended varieties: Champion, Early Scarlet Globe, Cherry Belle, Burpee White, Crimson Giant. White Icicle is a popular long white type; roots are 5 inches long, and the radishes look just like their name. China Rose, which grows to 6 inches long, is one of several good winter varieties. (These slower growers are planted in summer to reach maturity in the cool fall months. Unlike the early radishes, they are good for storing and will provide you with radishes in the winter.)

PLANTING INSTRUCTIONS

When to plant: Sow seeds beginning as early in spring as ground can be worked, and at weekly intervals until warm weather approaches. Radishes are also a good fall and winter crop in mild areas.

How to plant: Sow seeds ½ inch deep, and thin them to 1 inch apart when tops are up. If you plant them in rows, leave 12 inches between the rows. Radishes like a loose, fertile soil.

CULTURE

Keep radishes growing rapidly with regular watering, and include some liquid fertilizer with one or two of your watering sessions.

INSECT PESTS

Root maggots, the only real enemy of the radish, do their damage by tunneling into the edible roots. Dust or spray with diazinon at the seedling stage. *Caution:* Do not apply this chemical once the plants' edible roots have started to swell.

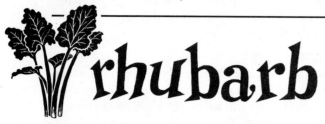

rhubarb

Wherever there is an odd corner, even in flower beds, there is a place for this handsome, bold-textured perennial. Unlike most vegetable crops, rhubarb takes kindly to either sun or partial shade. It is easy to grow, and — for some reason or other — the bugs seldom touch it!

CHARACTERISTICS

Rhubarb — one of the "big three" perennials along with artichoke and asparagus — won't do much until it has one growing season under its belt. After that, however, it will produce edible stalks each spring for up to 8 years, especially from the third year on.

It takes only 8 or 10 plants to supply the average family with all the rhubarb pie they can handle.

Caution: Never harvest the rhubarb leaves, as they are poisonous.

Regional considerations: Rhubarb does well in many garden situations, but it doesn't grow well in all sections of the country. It likes cool weather, and thrives in regions where winters are cold. Very little rhubarb is grown in the South because rhubarb needs a winter dormant period to do well.

Recommended varieties: MacDonald, Victoria, Valentine.

PLANTING INSTRUCTIONS

When to plant: Plant crowns in early spring or fall.

How to plant: Plant divisions or crowns. If planting in rows, leave 3 feet between crowns and 5 feet between rows. Water slowly and deeply.

CULTURE

Rhubarb likes plenty of water most of the time; however, go easy on the watering for several weeks during midsummer to encourage a short dormant season. After each harvest season, apply a complete fertilizer. If you live in an area where winters are harsh, apply a mulch in late fall (manure works very well). In mild-winter areas never mind the mulch, but give plants a supplementary fall feeding.

To harvest a petiole or leaf stalk, grasp it at the lower end, close to the main part of the plant; pull down and to one side so the petiole or stalk snaps off cleanly. Never take all the leaf stalks off a plant. Use only the stalks of rhubarb; leaves contain oxalic acid, a poisonous chemical.

INSECT PESTS

Rhubarb is remarkably free from pests and disease.

salsify

This little-known root vegetable looks something like a parsnip, yet its creamy white flesh tastes mighty like — of all things — an oyster. Grow as you would parsnips.

CHARACTERISTICS

Salsify (pronounced SAL-si-fee) is a long-season crop, taking some 150 days to grow to maturity from seed.

Regional considerations: This hardy vegetable can be grown in most regions of the U.S. In far northern states it is allowed to remain in the ground until the end of Indian summer to attain full size.

Recommended variety: Mammoth Sandwich Island is the popular favorite.

PLANTING INSTRUCTIONS

When to plant: Sow seeds as early as possible in spring.

How to plant: Work the soil to a depth of at least 18 inches so that it will be loose and crumbly. Sow the seed in drills 15 inches apart, covering with ½ inch of fine soil. When plants are about 2 inches high, thin them out to 3 inches apart.

Since salsify is a long-season crop, it should be intercropped with something fast, such as lettuce, spinach, radishes, or Swiss chard.

CULTURE

Salsify's cultural requirements are much the same as for parsnips.

Be careful when harvesting the roots. Don't pull them out of the ground too forcibly or you will break them.

INSECT PESTS

Salsify is seldom bothered by pests or diseases.

spinach

Spinach is a fast-growing, rather exacting leaf crop that must have cool weather — or bust! Because it just can't take long days and hot temperatures, it has given some ground in recent years to heat-resistant chard as a home garden favorite. But true spinach lovers will tell you: "All right, so it takes a little trouble. Isn't it worth it?"

CHARACTERISTICS

The best way to grow spinach is to intercrop it from time to time with slower-growing vegetables. If you prefer to grow it in rows, make several successive plantings; this way, you'll be able to enjoy spinach for dinner fairly frequently, despite its "here-today-gone-tomorrow" harvesting habits.

Although spinach can't be harvested on a cut-and-come-again basis, as can kale and chard, it grows faster than either of them (40-50 days).

Spinach makes a handsome edging or border plant in the vegetable garden.

New Zealand spinach is a succulent plant (not a true spinach) that endures heat and drought and can be grown in summer as a spinach-substitute. It has a low, spreading habit, suited to ground-covering and odd spaces. The long shoots can be removed as one needs them. The leaves and stems of this plant are sensitive to frost, but the roots are hardy and live through winter, sending out new shoots in spring. Greener, more tender leaves will result if some shade and a little extra water is given the plants in warm regions. It grows much more slowly than true spinach (70 days from seed to maturity).

Regional considerations: Spinach is grown in most sections of the U.S.

Recommended varieties: Bloomsdale Long Standing, Nobel, Hybrid No. 7, Viking, America.

PLANTING INSTRUCTIONS

When to plant: Sow seeds in early spring and again in late summer. Make several successive plantings about 10 days apart, sowing only a few feet of row at a time. In mild-climate regions, sow in fall for a winter crop.

How to plant: Sow seeds ½ inch deep and 2 inches apart, in rows 18 inches apart. After seedlings start growing, remove excess seedlings so plants are spaced 8 inches apart.

The soil for spinach should be light, rich, moist, and finely worked. A dry surface mulch is beneficial, but the soil in contact with the seed, whose absorbent outside covering quickly dries out, must be uniformly moist.

CULTURE

Give spinach plenty of water. Overhead sprinkling is preferable to furrow irrigation.

Quick fertilizers, particularly those with a high nitrogen content, are especially valuable for spinach. Try one of the liquid fertilizers.

INSECT PESTS

Spinach leaf miner is a serious pest in many areas, particularly in spring. Larvae or maggots tunnel within the leaves, serpentine fashion; in extreme cases, they can defoliate the plants. Spray with diazinon or sevin, but discontinue spraying a safe period prior to maturity of spinach, as directed by manufacturer.

Occasional infestations of aphids, or of vegetable weevil (Southern states), can be controlled by spraying or dusting with rotenone.

SQUASH

Most home gardeners must practice a good deal of self control when considering squash, for many varieties are space-eaters of the first order. However, there is a thrill in growing this vegetable that no beginner should miss. (Growing squash is one of the best ways to spark a child's interest in gardening.) Some kinds grow rapidly and produce an abundance of small fruits. Others take several months to get where they're going, but their ultimate products are as big as watermelons.

CHARACTERISTICS

Squash — like melons and cucumbers — are a vine crop and a member of the cucurbit family (grow one and you can grow 'em all). There is nothing difficult about growing them, although they are a bit more exacting as to soil moisture than some vegetables.

When you think of squash, you generally think of two basic types: 1) the smaller-fruited, fast-growing summer types, most of which mature from seed in 50 to 65 days, and 2) the bigger, slower-growing winter varieties which take up to 120 days.

Summer squash, to be at its best for the dinner table, should be picked and used before fruits are fully grown (you should be able to pierce the skin of a young and tender squash by barely exerting pressure with your thumbnail). Summer squash grows on bushy, compact plants that don't take up too much space and, therefore, are well suited to small home gardens. All summer squash varieties are heavily productive over a fairly long period of time, and none more so than the great Western favorite, zucchini. In warm weather a bush of zucchini grows so fast it startles you. After blooming, the fruit forms so rapidly that you must inspect the

vines every day or two or the fruit will be too large. If you like to come staggering out of the garden with proof of your prowess to show one and all, plant 3 hills of zucchini!

Winter squash, with its large, hard-shelled fruits, is planted so it will ripen in the fall. Plants are of the runner type, and take up too much space for the average sized home garden. Unlike summer squash, fruits should be left on the vine until fully ripe, picked before first frosts arrive, and stored in a warm dry place for winter use.

Pumpkins, although not full-fledged squash in the true sense of the word, are a close cousin. Seeds should be planted only ½ inch deep; otherwise plant them, grow them, and harvest them as you would winter squash. Or, try the old-fashioned method of interplanting with corn. (For special techniques on growing real whoppers, see the chapter on novelty vegetables.)

Regional considerations: Squash is grown in most sections of the U.S. If your region does not have at least half-days of full sunshine, or if there are extremes of summer fog and wind, the growing of squash is not worthwhile.

Recommended varieties: *Summer squash:* Summer Crookneck, Early Prolific Straightneck, White Bush Scallop, Zucchini, Cocozelle, Zucco, Hyrific, Hybrid Zucchini, Chefini, Greyzini. *Winter squash:* Buttercup, Butternut, Hubbard, Banana, Royal Acorn. *Pumpkin:* Connecticut Field, Small Sugar, Big Max.

PLANTING INSTRUCTIONS

When to plant: Plant seeds 1 or 2 weeks after average date of last frosts. The planting dates for corn may be generally followed for squash. The squash is very tender and seed will fail in cold ground.

How to plant: The planting techniques discussed at some length in the chapter on melons are equally applicable to squash. However, there are some differences in the spacing requirements of squash.

Bush type summer varieties should be planted 2 feet apart in rows; if planted in hills, allow 4 feet from the center of one hill to the center of the next.

Runner-type winter varieties need 5 feet between plants if planted in rows, but require an 8 by 8-foot space if planted in hills.

Growing squash on rocks keeps them dry, helps to prevent rot. If vines are trained against fence, platforms for large squashes can prevent sagging.

CULTURE

Squash needs lots of water, enough to keep the root zone continually moist. Build a dike around the planting to hold water so it will soak down to the roots. The plants may suffer, however, if water covers their crowns. Get around this by doing all your watering in one place and training the vines elsewhere. You can sow the seeds in the middle of a circular irrigating dike about 2 feet across, and let the main part of the vines spread out beyond the dike. Or sow along a slightly raised furrow, then

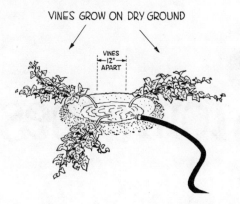

water in a depression along one side of the furrow and train the vines in the other direction.

Another way to avoid rotting of fruit on wet soil is to cover the entire vine area with a thin black plastic film (available at many nurseries). This black film stops all weed and grass growth, and keeps the fruit clean and dry. You simply slit holes in the film for the seeds and for water. The film warms the soil, speeds growth, and allows early planting.

Squash benefits from a 6-inch-deep straw or pine needle mulch laid around young plants. It helps to hold in soil moisture, and reduces rotting of fruit.

Liquid fertilizer, applied after the plants are 4 inches high and repeated every 6 weeks until the plants begin to bear, will hasten growth, increase the yield, and improve both the size and quality of the fruit.

For extra-early squash, try starting seed indoors in compressed peat pots. Set them out — pots and all — shortly before frosts are due to end, and give them a protective covering such as hotcaps.

If the vines run too heavily to leaf and stem (this can be caused by too much nitrogen) pinch back the tops. This may be necessary 2 or 3 times during the season.

Planting seed around cans which have been sunk in the ground conserves water and facilitates irrigation. Punch holes in the cans — water will gradually be released through them to the plant roots.

INSECT PESTS

Striped cucumber beetle and pickleworm are two common pests. See the section on cucumbers.

Additionally, squash bug and squash vine borer can cause serious damage to squash. These are difficult to control, but some success can be obtained by spraying young plants at 10-day intervals with diazinon and sevin, alternating sprays.

tomatoes

Best-tasting tomatoes in the world, most gardeners agree, are those you grow yourself. Although you may not be an ambitious vegetable grower, chances are you have room for a few tomato plants, even on a small lot. Tomatoes are easy to grow, and they will succeed in almost any kind of soil. Their brightly colored, juicy product is always in demand for summer salads and sandwiches, and the inevitable surplus can always be used for canning and preserves.

CHARACTERISTICS

If you've checked around the neighborhood for advice on growing tomatoes, you've probably heard something like this: "We don't do anything special. They just seem to grow like weeds." And then the next person may say, "It's all in the way we feed and spray them."

Actually, it's pretty hard to go far astray if you use good gardening sense. But you can have a really topnotch crop if you learn the plants' basic needs and give them a little extra care.

Tomatoes are tender, warm-weather plants that need a long, frost-free growing season (2 to 3 months, depending on variety, from the time plants are set out). They are deep rooted and will grow in most soils if drainage is good. The roots often go more than 6 feet deep.

It takes only 5 or 6 plants to meet the needs of the average family. (A dozen plants should supply bountiful tomatoes for the tomato-eatingest family imaginable.) For this reason, many home gardeners buy just a few young plants from a nursery (for about a nickel apiece) rather than bother with seeds. However, since nurseries usually carry only 2 or 3 varieties in seedling form, tomato enthusiasts and garden hobbyists prefer to scout seed racks in search of new or unusual kinds to try.

Regional considerations: Tomatoes are widely grown throughout the U.S. The one all-important climate consideration is ample warmth and sunshine during the growing season. If you live in an area where long periods of foggy weather are common in the summertime, or where cool nights are frequent, you would be better off not to grow tomatoes. The growth of the vines is not affected, but the fruits ripen very slowly.

Recommended varieties: The most ardent seed hobbyist will have his work cut out for him when he opens up his catalogs and starts running his eyes down the lists of tomato varieties. Seedsmen and nurserymen admit that they would gladly drop many old varieties which are inferior in production, disease resistance, and quality. Unfortunately, home gardeners have developed sentimental attachments to them. Here are some of the newer, yet proven varieties which seedsmen and advanced amateur gardeners rate highly: *Very early:* Fireball, Burpee's Big Early Hybrid, Early Giant Hybrid, Tiny Tim (miniature). *Midseason:* Jim Dandy Hybrid, Moreton Hybrid, Superman, Pearson (West), Floradel (South and East), Golden Jubilee, Red Cherry (cocktail size), San Marzano, Porter (pink, heat resistant). *Large fruit:* Burpee's Big Boy, Ponderosa (needs warm nights to set fruit). These new varieties are just as good eating as old favorites such as Marglobe, Rutgers, Earliana, and Stone, and have the ability to produce better yields under adverse conditions.

PLANTING INSTRUCTIONS

When to plant: Set out nursery transplants or young home-grown plants after all frost danger is past. If growing your own from seed, start them indoors 6 to 8 weeks before the average hard frost and plant them out when they are 6 to 10 inches tall. If you live in a mild-climate area, you can have a late fall crop if you make a second planting in early August.

How to plant: Tomatoes should be planted in a sunny location. They are not fussy about soil, but you'll get better results if you spade in generous amounts of well-rotted or processed manure prior to planting.

Also, scatter a light "snow" of balanced fertilizer over the bed, and work it in.

Tomatoes transplant easily, with little setback. However, when planting tomatoes, don't follow the general rule of setting plants at the same level they were in the nursery container or growing ground. Tomatoes should be planted deeply; you can bury as much as half to three-quarters of the stem because roots will form all along the buried portion.

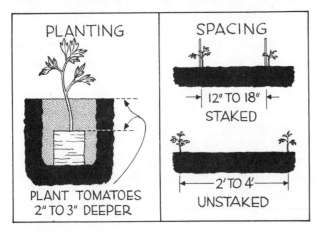

Water in the plants, and shade them with shingles or a portable lath cover for a few days if it's hot or windy. In colder areas you may have to protect them from the possibility of a surprise late frost.

If you start your own plants from seed, don't plant an entire flat unless you wish to grow several dozen plants. Plant seeds ½ inch deep in individual compressed peat pots and set them out — pots and all —

at planting time. Tomatoes are also easy (and fun) to start in one of the several types of pre-seeded containers that have become widely available and quite popular in recent years.

There are different opinions on just about every phase of growing tomatoes, but you'll find the widest divergence on the question of staking. Actually, there are no complications — it is largely a matter of personal choice. It is less work to let the plants grow naturally. However, if the plants are raised off the ground, fruits are cleaner, they get more warmth and ripen earlier, and plants take up less space. Staked plants can be set as close as 24 to 30 inches, whereas unstaked plants need 3 to 5 feet to spread.

CULTURE

Tomato plants need ample moisture during the growing season, but overwatering may stimulate too much leaf growth, cause the plant to drop some of its blossoms, and make the ripening fruit rather tasteless. If the soil is poorly drained, the roots may rot and the plants may die. Since the deep root system can search out moisture, the plants can coast along for some time after a deep watering. If you have adobe soil, you should only water every 3 or 4 weeks.

It is a good idea to cultivate occasionally to keep weeds from growing around plants. Use a light touch, however, or you will disturb the feeder roots near the soil surface.

Some gardeners try to push their plants along by

Cutting off the side sucker growth forces energy into the main stem. It is best to nip out the young sucker buds before they get this large.

As tomato plant grows, tie stem to stake with loops of raffia or twine. When stem reaches top of the stake, pinch out the tip to force side branching.

feeding frequently with a high nitrogen fertilizer. However, feeding during the early part of the season with a fertilizer high in nitrogen may force out leaf growth at the expense of fruit set.

Other gardeners get good results by feeding plants 2 or 3 times during the season with a fertilizer high in phosphorus, placing it in a ring 4 to 6 inches around each plant, then watering.

Although gardeners do get good results with either of these fertilizing methods, there is strong evidence that if the plants are set out in a well prepared, fairly rich soil, no other fertilizer is needed to get a respectable crop. Gardeners who follow this plan spread manure over the bed in fall after the old plants have been pulled up, then let it over winter on the bed until the next spring.

Experienced gardeners have come up with ingenious ways to train tomatoes: against a sunny wall, in large tubs on a trellis, up the sides and across the top of the inside of a greenhouse, or on small folding ladders. Remember, the support must

be strong enough to bear the weight of the plant when it becomes fruit-laden.

Here is a reliable staking method: You will need 2 x 2 stakes, 8 feet long, cedar or redwood. Sink them 18 inches deep into the ground beside each plant. Remove all side sucker growth so the plant's energy will go into the main stem. When plants are about 15 inches high make the first tie, loosely attaching the main stem of the tomato plant to the stake with a loop of raffia. Once the plants begin to grow fast, remove side suckers every day or so. Each time the plants grow another 15 inches, make another tie to keep the stem from sagging. When a plant reaches the top of the stake, pinch out the growing tip of the main stem to force side branching.

Tomatoes may not set fruit if night temperatures drop below 55° for several hours, or if day temperatures shoot up to 100°. If your plants turn out to be shy about bearing and drop their buds, better use one of the commercial fruit or bud-setting hormones when you grow tomatoes next year. The job

---

FOLDING SUPPORT FOR TOMATOES

This ladder-type trellis for supporting tomato vines is sturdy, attractive, and easy to store. To make each two-section trellis of the size shown here, you will need:

Legs — Four 1 by 3-inch boards, cut 2½ feet long.

Rungs — Three ¾-inch dowels, 18 inches long; and three ¾-inch dowels, 16⅝ inches long.

"Hinges" — Two ¾-inch dowels, 1⅝ inches long. The ladders shown here are about 2½ feet high. However, you can make them taller or spread them wider to accommodate larger plants and to straddle water basins. Their use need not be limited to tomatoes; they are also handy for supporting cucumbers, small melons, and other vining plants. Make the ladders as shown in the sketch. Space rungs 7

inches apart. Short dowels hold the legs together at the top. Paint the finished trellis green to blend with the foliage.

JEANNETTE GROSSMAN

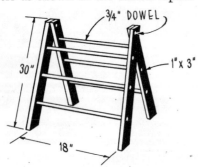

When tomatoes are through bearing, ladders fold easily for winter storage. Design: James K. Fudge.

of spraying the blossoms is easy, because many of these products come in sprayer-top cans.

INSECT PESTS

If you are the worrying kind, you may pass up growing tomatoes when you find out that tomato plants can be chewed, bitten, blighted, or rotted by over 30 different pests and diseases. However, you can now buy commercial tomato dusts and sprays containing insecticides and fungicides that will take care of the primary enemies. Follow the directions closely; generally, it is unsafe to use all-purpose pesticides on tomatoes when you intend to harvest within a week. If cutworms are a local problem, put out baits at planting time.

Turnips and rutabagas may not be as popular as two of their fellow root crops, carrots and beets — but those who do raise them constitute a loyal and enthusiastic following. Like other root crops, they are comparatively simple to grow.

CHARACTERISTICS

Turnips are a hardy vegetable and a cool-season grower. Grow them as you would grow beets. Like beets, they are prized for their tops as well as for the roots. They are one of the more rapid-growing of the root crops, reaching maturity from seed in 45 to 60 days. White-fleshed varieties are more popular than yellows.

Rutabagas are closely related to turnips. The differences between the two vegetables are minor, their taste is much the same, and their cultural requirements are similar. Rutabagas take about a month longer to mature. In mild-climate areas, many gardeners grow them in the fall and leave them in the ground to pull as needed during the winter months. The rutabaga is an indispensable accompaniment to a turkey dinner in many homes, particularly at Thanksgiving.

Regional considerations: Grown in most sections of the U. S.

Recommended varieties: *Turnips:* Purple-Top White Globe, Just Right, Shogoin (prized especially for its tops; especially popular in the South), Golden Ball (best of the yellow varieties). *Rutabagas:* American Purple Top, Burpee's Purple Top Yellow.

PLANTING INSTRUCTIONS

When to plant: As early in spring as ground can be worked. In the North, plant turnips again in midsummer for fall use. In the South and in the mild-climate areas of the West, plant again in fall and winter. In the Southeast, turnips for greens are usually spring-planted; turnips for roots and tops from late July through September.

How to plant: Sow seeds ⅛ inch deep in loose, rich, non-acid soil and in a sunny location. If planting in rows, leave 16 inches between rows. When plants are 3 inches tall, thin the rows so plants are 2 inches apart. (Rutabagas should be spaced a little farther apart than turnips.)

It's a good idea to sow only a portion of the seed packet at one time, so you won't have too many turnips at once. (Turnips, unlike rutabagas, become woody in a short while if they are left in the ground.) Make sowings every 4 weeks.

CULTURE

After thinning, give the young turnips some plant food to push them along to maturity faster.

Follow a regular watering program.

Don't try to store turnips — they give off a foul odor.

INSECT PESTS

Root maggots are the most common enemy. Treat the soil with sevin before planting seed.

Turnips and rutabagas are also subject to localized infestations of aphids, harlequin bugs, vegetable weevil, and cabbage looper, all of which can be effectively controlled with malathion or sevin (*note label precautions*).

if you seek the unusual

Like everything else in this world, the subject of vegetables has its lesser-known aspects. As a matter of fact, it has more than its share!

Here are just a few of the off-the-beaten-track possibilities that are discovered — sooner or later — by the true *aficionados* of vegetable gardening.

GOURDS — WHIMSICAL AND INEDIBLE

Gourds seem made to order for beginning gardeners: the large, flat seeds are easy to handle, and they germinate in a few days. These annual vines grow like Jack's beanstalk, and they produce their curious fruit in such abundance that they make even the newest gardener feel like an old pro.

From a packet of mixed gourd seed, you'll get a wide variety of shapes and colors; round, spoons, dippers, crook-necked, pears or Turk's turbans, yellows, greens, browns, plain, striped, or mottled with smooth or bumpy surfaces. They make wonderful toys (see the *Sunset* book, *Things to Make for Children*).

The fact that gourds are closely related to squash gives you a clue to their culture. Grow them as you'd grow summer squash. Let them climb on anything that's available — up a trellis or down a bank.

As the gourd flowers fade, it's fun to speculate on their eventual size, shape, and color, and watch the gourds begin to develop. They will ripen and color faster if you strip away some of the lush foliage to let the sun get at them. They are ready to harvest when they feel firm under pressure, with the skin reasonably hard and the stems beginning to shrivel and dry. The large fruited gourds (bottle, hercules club, dipper, crown of thorns) take longer to mature than the small fruited mixtures.

Store them in a cool dry place to season for a few weeks. If you rub gourds with several coats of floor wax, you can keep them for a month or more without having them mold. To keep them for indefinite periods of time, they must be thoroughly dried before covering with a protective coating.

POPCORN

Watch the way the kids take a sudden interest in the vegetable garden from the day you plant a few seeds of popcorn. You grow it just as you would grow regular sweet corn; the difference is in the end product and the harvesting. Ears are much smaller than sweet corn, usually 4 or 5 inches long and quite plump in appearance. Let them mature fully; then cut the stalks and put them where they can dry out. After shucking the ears, store the kernels in a dry place.

The hybrid popcorns expand in size 24 times when popped, and are exceptionally tender.

ORNAMENTAL CORN

Indian corn: As a feast for the eyes — not necessarily to eat — plant some Indian corn. The regular corn-sized ears, so useful in fall and winter arrangements, are made up of multicolored kernels in an endless variety of shades and patterns in red, yellow, orange, and black.

In some catalogs you'll find Indian corn listed under *Sweet corn* in the vegetable section; in others, it's listed as *Ornamental Corn* in the flower section. Also available are hybrids under such names as Rainbow corn and Crackerjack Hybrids, the latter a new brightly colored strain that can be eaten like sweet corn or used as popcorn.

Strawberry popcorn: It produces highly decorative, small, cone-shaped ears with shiny mahogany kernels. Ears somewhat resemble a 2-inch-long strawberry, or an overly fat loganberry. Straw colored husks are about 6 inches long. Plants grow to 3 feet.

GIANT PUMPKINS

It is no great trick to grow jumbo-sized pumpkins to delight your children at Hallowe'en. All it takes is a few simple procedures to come up with "monsters" that will put the store-bought kinds to shame.

Don't buy seeds of just any pumpkin. The varieties you can grow as big as 30 to 40 inches in diameter are called Connecticut Field and Big Max. Big Max pumpkins are enormous, but rather heart-shaped and with such thick flesh that they are hard to carve. Nonetheless, this is the variety that wins prizes at fairs! Plant seeds after the last frost, in mid-May or early June. Choose a sunny location for pumpkin vines. The plants grow large, so figure that a single planting will cover an area 10 to 20 feet in diameter.

Plant 6 to 8 seeds, 1 inch deep, within a circle 6

inches in diameter. If you want more than one set of vines, plant hills or clusters 8 feet apart. Water the seeds after planting. When the plants are 4 to 6 inches high, cut off the tops of all but two of the best plants in the circle.

Water the plants whenever you see signs of the slightest wilting in the leaves, but don't wet the foliage if you can help it, since this can encourage disease.

When you see small pumpkins 2 or 3 inches in diameter, remove all but 3 or 4 fruits on each vine. Or, for extra large pumpkins, remove all but one pumpkin from each vine. Remove fruits toward ends of vines; save those near the main stem. Keep removing later flowers.

Culture otherwise is much like that of winter squash (see chapter on squash). You can pick the pumpkins after they get hard, or leave them on the vines until just before Hallowe'en if it doesn't rain or freeze hard. If it begins to storm, harvest the pumpkins and put them in a cool (55° to 60°) spot. Leave stems attached to the pumpkins when you cut them.

PEANUTS

Growing your own goobers can be fun, and if you live in a mild climate that can provide the necessary growing season — 4 months of uninterrupted warm summer weather — they may be worth a try. Peanuts like a poor soil that is on the sandy-loamy side. They cannot take an acid soil.

The peanut is a sprawling plant with a many-branched stem. Its growing habits are curious and interesting; after the tiny female flowers open, the ovaries drop to the ground where they bury themselves (soil must be loose). The peanuts then begin to form underground. Even though full maturity may be reached in late summer or early fall, leave them in the ground; dig them after first frost.

SUNFLOWERS

Some seed stores group sunflowers with vegetable seeds; others on flower seed racks. They are a vegetable, albeit an unusual one. What really counts, though, is that here is a plant to fascinate your children. The stalks grow 7 to 12 feet high, and flower heads measure a foot or more across.

For best results, seeds should be planted at least 12 inches apart, to a depth of ½ inch, in moist, rich soil. You probably won't want more than 3 or 4 of them. (We know a family that was "strangely" bothered when a neighbor planted a whole row of sunflowers and the heads grew up above the fence dividing the two back yards. They had the uneasy feeling that they were being watched!)

Culture of sunflowers is very simple; just give them an occasional soaking. As seeds form in the sunflower heads, you'll notice that they attract birds (particularly bluejays). Place paper bags over the flowers if you wish to keep them intact.

When the seeds are ready to drop, children will enjoy picking them to eat as snacks. (Dry the seeds under a broiler; salt and cool.)

SWEET POTATO VINES

Do you like to watch plants grow? There aren't many that develop so rapidly or are as satisfying to watch as the sweet potato. All you have to do is push 3 toothpicks firmly into the potato at equal distances around the tuber, then lower the potato into the mouth of a jar or bowl of water so just the tip end is submerged. (It doesn't matter which end you leave up.) In about 10 days, little roots will begin to develop where eyes touch the water. As soon as there are a few good healthy roots, the sprouts will begin to elongate and the leaves unfold. In 6 weeks you'll have a lush vine.

The vine will grow for about 6 months or until the tuber shrivels. Then, start another one.

Like Irish potatoes, sweet potatoes don't return enough for the space they occupy in small gardens. If you'd like to experiment in growing them, start a potato as detailed above. After it has a root system, set it in the warm ground so that only the leaves are above the surface. Water it fairly often. If your summers are 4 to 5 months long, you can harvest a good crop come fall.

SOUTHERN PEAS (COWPEAS)

Once stereotyped as "Southern Cooking" along with cornbread and okra, Southern peas have climbed rapidly in popularity. Vines are large, robust, and spreading, resembling beans more than peas. They need warm weather to mature.

Pods splay out from upright stems like the fingers of a hand. While quite small they are eaten like snap beans, but they are usually allowed to mature to plump green stage for shelling.

Favorite kinds are Blackeye, Purple Hull, Brown Crowder, and Cream Pea, with many local varieties within each kind.

kitchen culture

Most fishermen remember the first fish they ever caught (at least they'll swear up and down that they do). If they *really* remember, chances are that it's because of their recollections of how the fish tasted when they — or more likely, Mom — prepared it for dinner.

It's the same way with a vegetable gardener. Once you've grown your own vegetables, you'll never forget how good they were.

Home grown vegetables are generally superior to market varieties for two reasons: 1) they can go from the garden to the dinner table in a matter of minutes rather than days or weeks, thus resulting in a minimum loss of truly fresh flavor and texture; and 2) home gardeners have the opportunity of growing all of the tastiest varieties — many of which the commercial growers must bypass because they lack certain qualities which make them difficult to grow in volume, to pack, to ship, or to store.

GIVE YOUR MENUS A LIFT

All of us get into a menu rut at times. Perhaps without thinking too much about it, we usually choose green peas to serve with fish; but artichokes, asparagus, broccoli, celery, spinach, or summer squash are good accompaniments, too. It's simpler to toss any vegetable with butter than it is to try out other seasonings and sauces.

The fact is, however, that the seasonings you use with vegetables make an important difference in the final taste appeal. A dash of lemon, a pinch of dill, a generous chopping of chives, or a hint of thyme or tarragon will change the flavor of some vegetables so subtly that what used to be a "no comment" dinner table item becomes a popular new favorite.

The sauce you mix with vegetables — sour cream, cheese, curry, soy, vinaigrette, Hollandaise, to mention a few — transforms them. Green beans, for example, taste completely different when sauced with either lemon butter, sour cream, tomato sauce, or soy.

On the following pages we present — in the fact-crammed, capsule fashion that only charts can make possible — the basic fundamentals in how to freeze your vegetable surpluses, how to cook vegetables and what to serve them with, and how to make use of the herbs that you grow in your garden.

FREEZING TECHNIQUES

1. Select vegetables that are barely mature, and freeze them as soon as possible after they have been picked.

2. Wash vegetables in cold water, preparing them just as you usually would for the table.

3. Most vegetables require blanching in boiling water to stop the action of enzymes that can cause off flavors and toughening. Use enough water to cover vegetables completely. Put not more than 2 pounds of a vegetable at one time in a wire basket or colander and immerse in briskly boiling water. Start counting blanching time when water returns to a boil — if this takes more than 2 minutes, blanch smaller quantities at a time. With a few vegetables, citric acid crystals (available in drug stores) or lemon juice should be added to blanching water to prevent darkening.

4. Lift vegetables from the boiling water and put at once into a pan containing ice and water. Chill only until vegetables are cool to the center (break one and test for chilling).

5. Remove from water, drain, and package. (Or freeze on trays and then pack.)

6. To package irregularly shaped products, put into a freezer bag, plunge the bag quickly into a deep pan of cold water, keeping top of bag well above surface of water. Twist top and fasten.

7. Freeze at once.

SOME FREEZE — SOME DON'T

Not all vegetables are well adapted for freezing. As a general rule, the cooking vegetables make best "freezers." These include asparagus, snap beans and lima beans, beets, cauliflower, broccoli, Brussels sprouts, peas, carrots, kohlrabi, rhubarb, squash, sweet corn, spinach and other greens. Vegetables that are frequently eaten raw, such as celery, cabbage, cucumbers, lettuce, onions, radishes, and tomatoes, generally do not freeze well.

Also, certain varieties of each vegetable will freeze better than others. If you intend to freeze large quantities of vegetables, write to one or more of the seed companies and ask for information as to the freezing characteristics of the varieties you prefer.

Vegetable	*How to prepare for freezing*
ARTICHOKES	Pull off coarse outer bracts. Cut about 1 inch off tops, and trim stems. Wash thoroughly. Blanching time: 8 to 10 minutes; add 3 teaspoons citric acid crystals or ½ cup lemon juice to every 2 quarts blanching water. Cool quickly, drain, and pack. **Note:** After blanching, artichokes may be stuffed with a filling such as cheese or bread crumbs before freezing.
ASPARAGUS	Asparagus toughens and loses flavor rapidly after harvest, so freeze promptly for best results. Trim stalks; use only tender portion. Wash. Blanching time: 2 to 4 minutes, depending on thickness of stalk. Cool quickly, drain, and pack.
BEANS, GREEN OR WAX	Select tender, stringless beans. Wash well and remove ends. Cut in 1-inch lengths or slice lengthwise (French-cut). Blanching time: 1½ minutes. Cool quickly, drain, and pack.
BEANS, LIMA	Remove beans from pods. Wash and sort for size. Blanching time: 2 to 3 minutes, depending on size. Cool quickly, drain, and pack.
BEETS	**For small tender whole beets,** wash and peel. Blanching time: 5 minutes. **For mature beets,** wash, cook until tender, then peel; slice or dice before freezing. Cool quickly, drain, and pack.
BROCCOLI	Wash thoroughly. Trim off large leaves and woody stem ends. Cut to serving size pieces. Split large stalks to ½-inch thickness. Blanching time: 2 to 3 minutes. Cool quickly, drain, and pack.
BRUSSELS SPROUTS	Trim off outer leaves. Wash well. Blanching time: 3 to 4 minutes. Cool quickly, drain, and pack.
CARROTS	Wash and scrape well. Cut in ⅓-inch dice. Very small carrots may be left whole. Blanching time: 2½ minutes for diced, 3 to 5 minutes for small whole carrots. Cool quickly, drain, and pack.
CAULIFLOWER	Wash, and break into serving size pieces. Blanching time: 3 minutes. Cool quickly, drain, and pack.
CELERY	Use crisp, tender celery. Trim, cut into 1-inch lengths. Blanching time: 3 minutes. Cool quickly, drain, and pack. **Note:** Frozen celery can be used only in cooked dishes.
CHINESE CABBAGE	Discard outside leaves, cut off stems. Cut through center of each stalk half way up stalk. Next, cut both stalk portions and upper leaf portions into 2-inch wedges. Blanching time: 1 minute for leafy parts, 1½ minutes for stalk portions. Cool quickly, drain, pack.
CHIVES	Wash and chop. Blanching not necessary. Package in small containers that are easy to open to remove small portions. **Note:** Use frozen chives within 2 months.
CORN	Use slightly immature yellow varieties of corn with fully developed kernels. Husk and de-silk. **For corn-on-the-cob,** blanching time: 5 to 8 minutes. Cool thoroughly, drain, package in freezer bags or wrap each ear separately in freezer wrap. **For cut corn,** blanching time: 1½ minutes, on the cob. Chill thoroughly, then cut kernels from cob; pack.
EGGPLANT	Peel, slice in ⅓-inch slices, or dice. Blanching time: 4 minutes. To prevent darkening, dip in acid solution after blanching, using 1 tablespoon citric acid crystals or ½ cup lemon juice in 2½ pints cold water. Cool thoroughly, pack.
KOHLRABI	Choose young small roots 2 to 3 inches in diameter. Cut off tops. Wash, peel, and dice. Blanching time: 1½ minutes. Cool quickly, drain, and pack.
OKRA	Wash well and cut off stems. Blanching time: 2 minutes for small pods, 3 minutes for larger pods. Cool quickly, drain, pack.
PARSNIPS	Cut off tops, wash, and peel. Slice lengthwise in ½-inch-thick slices. Blanching time: 2 minutes. Cool quickly, drain, pack.
PEAS	Shell and sort peas; wash well. Blanching time: ½ to 1 minute. Cool quickly, drain, and pack.
PEPPERS, GREEN OR RED	Wash well. Remove stem and seeds. Cut in halves, slice, or dice. Do not blanch. Package in small containers for convenience. **Note:** Extra portions of canned pimientos can also be frozen.
RHUBARB	Wash but don't peel. Cut into ½- to 1-inch slices. Pack in containers, seal, and freeze. Or, if you want them long, wrap in freezer paper, cellophane, or aluminum foil.
SALSIFY	Same as parsnips.
SPINACH, OTHER GREENS	Use young tender leaves. Wash thoroughly. Blanching time: 1½ minutes. Cool quickly, drain, pack. (Use same directions for kale, chard, Chinese mustard greens, wild greens.)
SQUASH, SUMMER	Use young, tender squash. Wash and cut into ½-inch slices. Blanching time: 3 minutes. Cool quickly, drain, pack. (Frozen summer squash varieties are acceptable, but somewhat difficult to prepare without over-cooking.)
SQUASH, WINTER	Cut into chunks, peel, then cook until soft in small amount of water. Mash. Cool and pack.
TOMATOES	Can only be frozen as tomato puree for use in soups and sauces, or as tomato sauce.
TURNIPS AND RUTABAGAS	Cut off tops, peel, and dice. Blanching time: 1 minute. Cool quickly, drain, and pack.

Vegetables

Artichoke to Eggplant

Vegetable	How do you cook it?	The vegetable appetizer	If you are serving fish
Artichokes 1 each serving	Trim, boil whole in acidulated water, 30 to 50 minutes, or until tender.	Hot or cold; whole or diced hearts or bottoms, in cocktail.	With any white fish; serve whole, or the hearts or bottoms.
Asparagus 1 lb. serves 2	Boil or steam, whole or sliced; cook until tender-crisp—3 to 15 minutes.	Raw, with dunking sauce; or cooked and rolled in ham or smoked salmon.	With any fish or shellfish, hot or cold.
Beans, green or wax 1½ lbs. serves 6	Boil whole, split, sliced, or chopped, 10 to 25 minutes.	Cold with antipasto; also pickled whole, with dill.	Any fish or shellfish.
Beans, Lima 3 lbs. serves 4	Shell, boil 20 to 30 minutes.	With vinaigrette, or curry sauce.	Any fish, especially fried.
Beets 2 lbs. serves 4	Whole or shredded; boil, steam, or bake. Combine with celery.	Pickled with antipasto; stuffed as hors d'oeuvre.	Any fish; and smoked fish.
Broccoli 2 lbs. serves 4	Steam or boil 10 to 15 minutes. May cook thinly sliced stems separately.	With French dressing or vinaigrette as first course; raw as appetizer.	With any fish, or smoked fish, and shellfish.
Brussels Sprouts 1 lb. serves 4	Boil, whole or halved, 8 to 15 minutes.	Raw stuffed; or with dunking sauce.	With any fish, plain or smoked.
Cabbage 1 lb. serves 4	Shred and cook 4 to 8 minutes; or quarter and cook 6 to 10 minutes; or wilt with bacon.	Raw, stuffed with shellfish and mayonnaise, for hors d'oeuvre.	Any baked, steamed, fried, or broiled fish.
Cabbage, Red 1 lb. serves 4	Cook with apple, onion, and wine or vinegar.	Strips, raw, with dunking sauce.	Any fish — especially when cooked with red wine vinegar.
Carrots 1 lb. serves 4	Slivered, shredded, sliced, shaved, shoestring, or whole. Boil or steam.	Raw sticks with dunking sauce; or curls with relishes.	With any baked, steamed, broiled, or fried fish.
Cauliflower 1 large head serves 6	Whole, broken into flowerettes, or sliced; boiled or steamed 4 to 25 minutes.	Raw flowerettes with dunking sauce, such as guacamole or dill mayonnaise.	With any fish, especially smoked salmon.
Celery 1 large bunch serves 4	Raw, steamed, or braised, 10 to 18 minutes.	As a relish; stuffed; with dunking sauce.	Any fish or shellfish.
Chard 1 lb. serves 2	Steamed, 4 to 11 minutes.		Smoked fish, such as finnan haddie; any fish.
Chinese Cabbage 1½ lbs. serves 4	Slice crosswise—1-inch-thick slices at base, larger from leafy sections. Toss in hot oil; cover and steam just until tender-crisp, adding water if necessary.		With any fish or shellfish, especially with prawns.
Collards 2 lbs. serves 4	Cut off root ends. Steam in small amount of water until tender—10 to 15 minutes.	Sprinkle tenderest raw leaves with French dressing or vinaigrette as first course.	Any fish or shellfish.
Corn 1 or 2 ears serves 1	Boil or steam on the cob, 4 to 6 minutes; sauté off the cob; roast on cob, 10 to 20 minutes.	Raw, off the cob, with sour cream.	Roasted, with charcoal-broiled fish, and in pit cooking.
Cucumber 1 medium serves 2	Usually served raw, but may be cooked 5 to 10 minutes, fried, or stuffed and baked.	Sticks, with dunking sauce; in cups with cheese or fish filling.	With any fish, particularly raw and dressed with sour cream and dill.
Eggplant 1 medium serves 4	Fried, baked, boiled, steamed.	As caponata or "eggplant caviar."	With any white fish, simply cooked, or sauced with cheese and tomato.

If you serve meat or poultry	The vegetable in a salad	Good companions (to garnish, season, combine)	What will you sauce it with?
With veal, lamb, meat loaf, ham, chicken.	Whole, with mayonnaise; or hearts, with French dressing.	Garlic, olive oil, lemon juice, dill.	Melted butter, grated cheese, mayonnaise, Hollandaise, lemon juice.
With any — especially chicken, lamb, ham, veal, squab.	With vinaigrette, mayonnaise, or French dressing; also sliced in mixed green salad.	Dill, tarragon, lemon juice, nutmeg, parsley, chopped hard cooked egg, slivered almonds.	Butter, mayonnaise, vinaigrette, sour cream, Hollandaise, capers, almonds.
Any meat or poultry—or game.	Vinaigrette or mayonnaise in combination with French dressing.	Onion, garlic, bay, savory, dill, rosemary, thyme, nutmeg, chili powder, anchovies, mushrooms.	Butter, tomato sauce, sour cream, browned butter, soy.
Ham, pork, poultry.	In combination salads.	Parsley, savory, corn, chives, crisp bacon.	Cream sauce, sour cream, lemon parsley butter.
Tongue, veal, liver, lamb, meat loaf.	With cress and French dressing; or in combination with other vegetables.	Tarragon, dill, vinegar, mustard, caraway, cloves.	Dill sauce, lemon butter, sour cream, Béarnaise, vinaigrette.
Ham, pork, turkey, chicken, veal paprika—almost any meat.	With French dressing, mayonnaise, or vinaigrette.	Garlic, lemon, thyme, oregano, olive oil, chopped egg, slivered almonds, crisp bacon.	Lemon butter, sour cream, Hollandaise, cheese sauce, browned crumbs, slivered nuts, soy.
Ham, tongue, pork, turkey, duck, game.	Sliced, raw, in green salad; or slaw; cooked in combination salad.	Savory, oregano, vinegar, lemon, olive oil, onions, chestnuts, mushrooms.	Sour cream, lemon butter, beurre noir, soy.
Tongue, corned beef, lamb, liver, kidneys.	As cole slaw, or in mixed green salad with sour cream, mayonnaise, or French dressing.	Dill, caraway, curry, tarragon, oregano, paprika, onion, parsley, nutmeg.	Sour cream, lemon butter, or Béarnaise.
Pork, goose, beef Stroganoff, venison.	Cole slaw—may be in combination with green cabbage.	Caraway, dill, cloves, allspice, wine vinegar, red wine, apple.	Sour cream, lemon butter, Hollandaise, dill sauce.
With almost any, especially lamb, chicken, meat loaf, veal.	Grated raw in cole slaw or mixed green; cooked in combination salad.	Parsley, thyme, dill, cloves, ginger, mint, allspice, rosemary, garlic, brandy.	Lemon butter, parsley butter, dill sauce, soy.
Ham, lamb, beef, pork, meat loaf, game.	Cold, with vinaigrette; raw in combination salad; cooked, with curry mayonnaise.	Rosemary, parsley, savory, caraway, basil.	Sour cream, cheese sauce, vinaigrette, mayonnaise, parsley, Hollandaise, or lemon butter.
Beef, lamb, pork, chicken, duck, goose, ham, game.	Sliced thin in green salad; alone with French dressing or mayonnaise; braised in celery Victor.	Tarragon, parsley, caraway, rosemary, onion, chives, chili powder, almonds.	Cream sauce, sour cream, butter, cheese sauce, curry sauce, parsley butter.
With any meat or poultry, especially ham, tongue, or mutton.		Lemon, vinegar, bacon, oregano, garlic, onion, rosemary.	Soy, butter, bacon drippings, sour cream, lemon, parsley butter.
With any, especially with pork.	Tear leafy portions into green salad, fresh vegetable salad.	Bits of fried pork, garlic, vinegar.	Sweet-sour sauce, soy sauce, thin cornstarch-water sauce seasoned with soy sauce.
Any meat or poultry—or game.	Tenderest leaves raw, with vinaigrette or French dressing, or wilted with bacon drippings and vinegar.	Small bits of bacon, lemon juice, vinegar, toasted sesame seeds, nutmeg, dill, basil, tarragon.	Melted butter, lemon butter, cream sauce, soy sauce, sour cream, mushroom sauce, cheese sauce.
With almost any, especially pork, ham, poultry, sausage.	Cold, cooked, with pimiento and green pepper, mayonnaise.	Fresh ground pepper, chili powder, garlic butter, oregano.	Butter, herb butters, cream sauce when off cob.
Braised, with ham, tongue, liver, meat loaf.	In any mixed or combination salad; also sliced or shredded.	Chives, parsley, dill weed, dill seed, onion, burnet.	Sour cream, mayonnaise, dill sauce, parsley butter, soy, vinaigrette.
Mutton, lamb, meat loaf, shashlik, meat balls.		Basil, oregano, dill, rosemary, allspice, bay, savory, olive oil, cheese, bacon.	Tomato sauce, cheese sauce.

Vegetables

Endive to Zucchini

Vegetable	How do you cook it?	The vegetable appetizer	If you are serving fish
Endive 1 head serves 2 or 3	Raw, or braised until it is tender.	Stuffed with cheese or other savory fillings, or plain with dunking sauce.	Braised, with salmon, swordfish, lobster, shrimp.
Kohlrabi 1 medium-sized serves 1	Remove leaves, peel, cube or slice. Cook covered in small amount boiling salted water until tender.		With any fish.
Leeks 1 stalk serves 1	Braised until tender; boiled, 15 to 35 minutes.	Cold, cooked, with vinaigrette.	With any fish or shellfish.
Lettuce, Various 1 medium head serves 2 or 3	Usually raw. Shred and wilt, or braise until tender; stuff, roll and braise.	As a garnish, or stuffed and rolled.	Braised, with any fish or shellfish.
Okra 1 lb. serves 4	Boil whole or sliced, 8 to 20 minutes; sauté until tender; bake.	Cooked and marinated.	With any fish, especially steamed or baked; or shellfish.
Onions 1 lb. serves 3 or 4	Boiled whole, 15 to 40 minutes; baked; fried; French fried; braised.	Raw as relish; pickled.	With almost any fish, usually in stuffing or as seasoning.
Parsnips 1 lb. serves 2 or 3	Boiled; or parboiled and fried until tender.		With most sautéed or baked fish.
Peas ¾ lb. serves 1	Steamed or boiled.		With any and all fish and shellfish.
Peppers, Green 1 large serves 1 or 2	Raw; fried; stuffed and baked; steamed.	Raw strips, with dunking sauce.	With any fish or shellfish, usually as a seasoning.
Potatoes, White ½ lb. serves 1	Boiled; fried; baked; French fried; 20 to 40 minutes, or until tender.	Potato chips, with dunking sauce. Hot French fries.	With any fish or shellfish.
Radishes 1 bunch serves 2	Cook whole with or without tops, covered, in small amount boiling salted water until tender.	Raw, as relish, may be with dipping sauce.	Any fish or shellfish.
Rhubarb 1 lb. serves 4	Trim ends; cut in 1 to 2-inch pieces. Simmer, covered, with ⅓ cup water, ½ cup sugar for 1 pound rhubarb until tender		
Rutabagas ½ lb. serves 1	Boil 20 to 40 minutes; mash or not.	Raw, with dunking sauce.	
Salsify (Oyster plant) 1 lb. serves 2 or 3	Boil 15 to 35 minutes in acidulated water; parboil and sauté.	Raw, with dunking sauce.	Browned in butter with white fish.
Spinach or other greens 1 lb. serves 2	Steam until wilted.		With any fish or shellfish.
Squash, Winter 1 lb. serves 2	Boiled and mashed; baked until tender.		
Tomatoes 1 lb. serves 2	Raw; stewed; fried; or baked.	Raw, especially cherry tomatoes.	With any fish or shellfish.
Turnips 1 lb. serves 2	Boiled, and mashed, sliced, or diced.	Raw sticks with dunking sauce.	With white fish, dressed with lemon and parsley butter.
Zucchini (summer squash) 1 lb. serves 2	Boiled and mashed; sautéed or French fried.	Raw, with dunking sauce; cooked, vinaigrette.	With any fish.

If you serve meat or poultry	The vegetable in a salad	Good companions (to garnish, season, combine)	What will you sauce it with?
Braised with game, poultry, any or all meat.	Alone with French dressing, or in a mixed green salad.	Butter, bacon, tarragon, chives, basil.	Raw—French dressing. Cooked—cream sauce, Mornay sauce, mushroom sauce.
With lamb, pork, veal, beef, liver, sausage.		Snipped parsley, chives, celery seed.	Melted butter, cream sauce, cheese sauce.
With beef, mutton, liver, heart, and game.	Raw, shredded in mixed green salad; leeks Victor.	Bay, oregano, black pepper, parsley.	Cheese or caper sauce, sour cream, soy.
Braised, with any and all meats.	A must for almost any salad.	Parsley, chives, tarragon, chervil, blue cheese, any delicate herb.	French dressing, sour cream, mayonnaise, and all salad dressings.
With rabbit, ham, lamb, liver, kidney, poultry.	Cooked, cold, good with French dressing.	Onion, garlic, bay, lemon, parsley, thyme, green pepper.	Tomato sauce, melted butter.
With liver, steak, poultry, roasts, game—almost any meat.	Raw, with almost any salad.	Basil, sage, thyme, oregano, ginger, paprika, almonds.	Cream sauce, sour cream, mustard sauce, tomato sauce, melted butter.
With lamb, veal, liver, sausage, meat balls.		Lemon, butter, parsley.	Cream sauce, melted butter, browned crumbs.
With any and all meats, poultry, and game.	Cooked, in combination or Russian salad.	Basil, onions, mint, borage, marjoram, tarragon, thyme, cinnamon, cumin.	Cream, butter, parsley or lemon butter, sour cream.
With any meat or poultry, especially lamb, tripe, meat loaf.	Raw in any mixed salad, cole slaw, or combination salad; vinaigrette.	Garlic, olive oil, oregano, rosemary, onion, basil.	Butter, olive oil, tomato sauce.
With any meat, poultry, or game.	Cooked, for potato salad, and in herring and Russian salad.	Onion, garlic, basil, bay, parsley, chives, caraway, dill, sesame seeds, poppy seeds, thyme.	Cream, sour cream, cheese sauce, melted butter, herb sauce.
With any meat or poultry.	Raw, sliced thin or in slivers in green salads, vegetable salads, cole slaw.	Salt, pepper, caraway, chives.	Melted butter, sour cream, mayonnaise.
Serve chilled sauce with poultry, pork.		Brown sugar, nutmeg, mace, cinnamon, ginger, orange peel.	Whipped cream, sour cream, honey.
With goose, duck, pork, ham, sausage.		Dill seed or weed, parsley, rosemary, fennel, black pepper.	Butter.
With ham, veal, chicken, lamb.	Cooked, in combination salad.	Parsley, chives, thyme, black pepper, shallots, tarragon, almonds, filberts.	Cream sauce, cheese sauce, herb sauce, brown butter, soy, tomato sauce.
With ham, tongue, liver, or any meat or poultry.	Raw, in mixed green salad; wilted with bacon drippings.	Mushrooms, dill, nutmeg, bacon, basil, tarragon, lemon, hard cooked egg, vinegar.	Sour cream, mushroom or cheese sauce, cream sauce, soy, butter.
With any meat, poultry, or game, especially pork, turkey, venison, goose.		Cinnamon, allspice, dill, maple or brown sugar, cloves, chives, parsley.	Butter, browned butter, sausage or bacon drippings.
With beef, lamb, mutton, chicken, ground meats, hash, sausage.	Sliced, plain, with lettuce; or in most combination salads.	Onion, green pepper, garlic, basil, black pepper, oregano.	Olive oil, French dressing, sour cream, mayonnaise, salad dressing.
With most meats and poultry, especially duck, goose, lamb, mutton, turkey.		Dill weed, onion, rosemary, basil, black pepper, fennel.	Butter.
With sausage, ham, liver, lamb, meat loaf, pork.	Sliced raw in salad; cooked with vinaigrette.	Garlic, lemon, olive oil, dill, oregano, fennel, caraway.	Tomato sauce, sour cream, melted butter, mushroom sauce.

Basic Herbs

	Appetizers	Eggs	Fish — Shellfish
BASIL *Annual, 1 ft., tender. Purple form also. Mild flavor of anise and spice, slight mint aftertaste*	Tomato juice cocktail. (Basil and tomatoes are natural partners.) Stuffed eggs	All egg dishes. Tomato sauce for omelets. Cheese soufflé or fondue	In liquid used to cook fish or shellfish. Fish loaves. In basil butter to serve with fish. In stuffings. Cioppino
BAY *Sweet bay or laurel, evergreen tree, handsome in garden, tubs. Strong aromatic, pungent flavor*	Use sparingly in hot tomato juice or bouillon. Add to corned beef, ham when cooking meats for cold plates		In court bouillon for cooking fish. With smoked fish. Fish chowders. With shrimp. (Use lightly)
DILL *Annual, 3 ft., finely cut thread-like leaves, yellow bloom. Sharp, aromatic, caraway-like flavor*	(Minced fresh leaves or seeds.) In Louis dressing for crab. With smoked or pickled fish. In cheese spreads		Fish sauces such as tartar sauce or cream sauce. Place cut leaves over fish, let stand few minutes, remove, broil
MARJORAM *Perennial, 2 ft., leaves gray-green, purple blooms. Sweet, spicy flavor, mint aftertaste*	Stuffed mushrooms or sautéed mushrooms. With cottage cheese or cream cheese	Only in sauces to go with eggs, such as sharp Cheddar cheese sauce	Creamed fish dishes. Sauces for steamed fish. Fish stuffing. Cioppino. Sprinkled on fish, baked or broiled, when cooked
MINT *Hardy perennial; spearmint is best known. Refreshing, fruity, aromatic flavor*	Hot or cold fruit or wine beverages. Fruit cocktails		As garnish for any fish
OREGANO *Wild marjoram (Origanum vulgare), perennial, 2½ ft. Strong clove flavor, slightly bitter*	In guacamole (avocado dip). Sprinkled over pizza. In mushroom dishes. (Often called the mushroom herb.)	In Spanish sauces for omelets, baked eggs, or poached eggs. Very light sprinkling on soft cooked eggs	Spanish sauces for fish. Cioppino. Fish stuffings. Oregano butter to serve with fish. Louis dressing
PARSLEY *Biennial or perennial, 1 ft. Curled or plain leaves. Sweet, spicy, rather peppery flavor*	Mince and use as garnish for canapés. Mix into spreads. Add to cocktail biscuits. Combines with all herbs	All egg dishes (add at last minute to prevent darkening). Use as both seasoning and garnish	Always in court bouillon. Parsley butter to serve with fish. Tartar sauce. Fish stuffings
ROSEMARY *Hardy shrub, 3 ft., blue flowers, grayish leaves. Pungent, piny, resinous flavor; quite aromatic*	Jams and jellies. In tiny biscuits with ham filling. Fruit cocktail if removed before serving		Only in stuffings for strong flavored fish such as salmon
SAGE *Shrubby perennial, 2 ft., gray leaves, purple bloom. Fragrant. Aromatic, slightly bitter flavor*	In cheese spreads; on cheese-topped canapés. Sage-seasoned pastry wrapped around cooked sausage meat and baked	Small pinch in cheese soufflé. In cheese sauces for eggs	Small amount in stuffings for fish
SAVORY *Both annual and perennial forms, 15 to 18 inches. Attractive plant. Warm, aromatic, resinous flavor*	Tomato juice cocktail. Marinated beans, both dry and green. In tiny cocktail biscuits	All egg dishes (a mild herb). Cheese soufflé	Fish chowders. Cream sauce for salmon loaf with onion or chives. Fish stuffings. Baked or broiled fish
TARRAGON *Perennial, 2 ft.; should cut leaves, tops, often. Aromatic, licorice-anise flavor, slightly bitter*	Tomato juice cocktail. Fish cocktail. Tarragon butter for canapés	All egg dishes if used lightly	All fish and shellfish dishes, but use lightly. Tarragon butter or sauces. Marinades for broiled or barbecued fish
THYME *Shrubby perennial, 1 ft., gray-green leaves, purple flowers. Strong, warm, clove-like flavor*	Blended with strong cheeses. Tomato juice cocktail. Sauerkraut juice or mixed vegetable juices	Scrambled or baked eggs if used cautiously. Cheese sauce for eggs	All fish and shellfish. Chowders, gumbos, bouillabaisse. Fish stuffings. Sauces or thyme butter to serve with fish

Meat — Game	*Poultry*	*Salads*	*Soups*	*Vegetables*
With beef, liver, veal, lamb, pork. Any dish using tomato sauce. Spaghetti. Meat marinades. Stuffings	All poultry stuffings. Stewed or fricasseed chicken or rabbit. Sprinkle on all poultry before roasting	Tomato aspic. French dressings with tomato base. In vinegar. Sprinkle over sliced tomatoes, cucumbers	Tomato soup, minestrone, split pea soup, spinach soup, bouillon	Tomatoes in any form, carrots, summer squash, eggplant, green beans. Italian dishes, including pastas and rice
Tongue, beef pot roasts or stews. Corned beef and corned pork. Kidneys, heart. Spaghetti	Chicken fricassee or stewed chicken. (Use lightly)	Tomato aspic (heat in juice, then discard). Cook fish with it for fish salads	Vegetable beef soup, chicken broth, borsch, split pea soup	Artichokes (small piece in cooking water). In boiled potatoes, pickled beets With vegetables around roast
Broiled chops and steaks, lamb chops, after cooking one side; remove before serving. Corned meats. Lamb sauce	Creamed chicken. Sweetbreads	With sour cream over cucumbers. Pickled beets. Finely cut leaves or seeds in potato salad. Tossed green salad	Fish soups and chowders. Small pinch in vegetable soups	Sprinkle on potatoes browned in butter. Small amount in peas. Add to green beans, cabbage, cauliflower
Lamb (all cuts), beef, veal. Steak and kidney pie. Venison marinades. In slits in venison roast. Rabbit or game birds	Rub lightly over skin and cavity before broiling. Stuffings. Goose. Fricassees	Tossed green salads with chives and French dressing. (Fresh leaves do not need mincing)	Onion soup, bouillon, clam chowder, mushroom soup	Zucchini, stuffed vegetables, cooked celery, mushrooms, peas, carrots, spinach, fried potatoes
Lamb accompaniment, sauce or jelly. Mint chutney for lamb curry. Stick in slits in leg of lamb. Also with veal	Garnish	Fruit salads or in simple syrup used to marinate fruit. Apple salad. Garnish	Fresh pea soup	Carrots, peas, green beans, cabbage slaw, new potatoes. (Add just before serving so it won't darken)
Spaghetti sauces. All game. Mushroom sauce for steak or meat loaf. Mexican dishes. Goose. Meat marinades	All game birds. Stuffings for goose, duck, or turkey	Avocado salad. Marinated green beans, garbanzos, Mexican beans	Mushroom, spinach, vegetable, lentil soups	Add to all mushroom dishes to strengthen flavor. Spanish sauces for vegetables. Green beans, onions
All braised dishes, stews. In savory butters for steak sauce. Stuffings. Garnish	Use inside poultry when baking without stuffing. In stuffings, as seasoning for stock, fricassees. Garnish	For green mayonnaise to serve with salads. Cut up into salads or add to dressings at last minute	In practically all soups for both flavor and garnish. In tiny dumplings or other soup accessories	In or over all vegetables. With rice or spaghetti. Lemon butter for potatoes, carrots, asparagus
Veal or lamb (insert in slits in roast). Pork and beef dishes. Italian dishes. Called the meat herb	All chicken dishes (but use lightly). Wine marinades or basting sauces. In stuffings instead of sage. Rabbit	In water used to cook chicken for salad. Do not chop into fresh salads because flavor is better when cooked	Minestrone, small pinch in chicken, pea, or spinach soups	Cabbage, broccoli, Brussels sprouts. Boiled or baked potatoes. Turnips. (Use sparingly)
Sausage, pork (all cuts), veal, lamb. Stuffings. Duck	In stuffings for all poultry (be sure it is not stale or it may be bitter). Use 1 leaf in chicken gravy			Stuffings for vegetables. Onions. Eggplant with cheese
Sweetbreads, brains, kidneys. Smoked turkey. Pork. Veal. Lamb shanks	All poultry stuffings. Rub over poultry before broiling. Fricassees. Savory butter to baste roasting birds	Bean salads (known as bean herb). Tossed salads with tomato	Bean, lentil, split pea soups.	All kinds of beans, peas, cabbage, sauerkraut, rice, lentils, summer squash, artichokes
Particularly good with veal. Rabbit. Tarragon butter for steaks. (Don't use this herb too often)	With all poultry if used cautiously. Wine marinades. Chicken livers with sour cream	In vinegar. With cucumbers, crab, shrimp. Pinch in sour cream dressing. Vinegar greatest use	Chicken or fish soups and chowders. (Only a pinch)	Vinaigrette sauce for asparagus, artichokes. Hollandaise. Cauliflower marinated in tarragon vinegar
With all meats, if used with restraint. Game. Tomato sauces. Liver, kidneys. Duck	Included in most poultry seasonings. Fricassees. Duck	Tomato aspic. Cabbage slaw. Minced or crumbled over sliced tomatoes. Pickled beets	Tomato soup, minestrone, clam chowder, gumbo, split pea soup	Beans, peas, spinach, zucchini, onions, tomatoes, carrots

INDEX

AVERAGE HARD-FROST DATES*

Based on U.S.D.A. weather records

State	Last in Spring	First in Fall	State	Last in Spring	First in Fall	State	Last in Spring	First in Fall
Alabama, N. W.	Mar. 25	Oct. 30	Kentucky	Apr. 15	Oct. 20	N. Dakota, E.	May 16	Sept. 20
Alabama, S. E.	Mar. 8	Nov. 15	Louisiana, No.	Mar. 13	Nov. 10	Ohio, No.	May 6	Oct. 15
Arizona, No.	Apr. 23	Oct. 19	Louisiana, So.	Feb. 20	Nov. 20	Ohio, So.	Apr. 20	Oct. 20
Arizona, So.	Mar. 1	Dec. 1	Maine	May 25	Sept. 25	Oklahoma	Apr. 2	Nov. 2
Arkansas, No.	Apr. 7	Oct. 23	Maryland	Apr. 19	Oct. 20	Oregon, W.	Apr. 17	Oct. 25
Arkansas, So.	Mar. 25	Nov. 3	Massachusetts	Apr. 25	Oct. 25	Oregon, E.	June 4	Sept. 22
California			Michigan, Upper Pen.	May 25	Sept. 15	Pennsylvania, W.	Apr. 20	Oct. 10
Imperial Valley	Jan. 25	Dec. 15	Michigan, No.	May 17	Sept. 25	Pennsylvania, Cen.	May 1	Oct. 15
Interior Valley	Mar. 1	Nov. 15	Michigan, So.	May 10	Oct. 8	Pennsylvania, E.	Apr. 17	Oct. 15
Southern Coast	Jan. 15	Dec. 15	Minnesota, No.	May 25	Sept. 15	Rhode Island	Apr. 25	Oct. 25
Central Coast	Feb. 25	Dec. 1	Minnesota, So.	May 11	Oct. 1	S. Carolina, N. W.	Apr. 1	Nov. 8
Mountain Sections	Apr. 25	Sept. 1	Mississippi, No.	Mar. 25	Oct. 30	S. Carolina, S. E.	Mar. 15	Nov. 15
Colorado, West	May 25	Sept. 18	Mississippi, So.	Mar. 15	Nov. 15	S. Dakota	May 15	Sept. 25
Colorado, N. E.	May 11	Sept. 27	Missouri	Apr. 20	Oct. 20	Tennessee	Apr. 10	Oct. 25
Colorado, S. E.	May 1	Oct. 15	Montana	May 21	Sept. 22	Texas, N. W.	Apr. 15	Nov. 1
Connecticut	Apr. 25	Oct. 20	Nebraska, W.	May 11	Oct. 4	Texas, N. E.	Mar. 21	Nov. 10
Delaware	Apr. 15	Oct. 25	Nebraska, E.	Apr. 15	Oct. 15	Texas, So.	Feb. 10	Dec. 15
District of Columbia	Apr. 11	Oct. 23	Nevada, W.	May 19	Sept. 22	Utah	Apr. 26	Oct. 19
Florida, No.	Feb. 25	Dec. 5	Nevada, E.	June 1	Sept. 14	Vermont	May 23	Sept. 25
Florida, Cen.	Feb. 11	Dec. 28	New Hampshire	May 23	Sept. 25	Virginia, No.	Apr. 15	Oct. 25
Florida, South of Lake Okeechobee, almost frost-free			New Jersey	Apr. 20	Oct. 25	Virginia, So.	Apr. 10	Oct. 30
Georgia, No.	Apr. 1	Nov. 1	New Mexico, No.	Apr. 23	Oct. 17	Washington, W.	Apr. 10	Nov. 15
Georgia, So.	Mar. 15	Nov. 15	New Mexico, So.	Apr. 1	Nov. 1	Washington, E.	May 15	Oct. 1
Idaho	May 21	Sept. 22	New York, W.	May 10	Oct. 8	W. Virginia, W.	May 1	Oct. 15
Illinois, No.	May 1	Oct. 8	New York, E.	May 1	Oct. 15	W. Virginia, E.	May 15	Oct. 1
Illinois, So.	Apr. 15	Oct. 20	New York, No.	May 15	Oct. 1	Wisconsin, No.	May 17	Sept. 25
Indiana, No.	May 1	Oct. 8	N. Carolina, W.	Apr. 15	Oct. 25	Wisconsin, So.	May 1	Oct. 10
Indiana, So.	Apr. 15	Oct. 20	N. Carolina, E.	Apr. 8	Nov. 1	Wyoming, W.	June 20	Aug. 20
Iowa, No.	May 1	Oct. 2	N. Dakota, W.	May 21	Sept. 13	Wyoming, E.	May 21	Sept. 20
Iowa, So.	Apr. 15	Oct. 9						
Kansas	Apr. 20	Oct. 15						

*Allow 10 days either side of above dates to meet local conditions and seasonal differences.